GOOD HOUSEKEEPING
FAMILY LIBRARY

MONEY-SAVING
COOK BOOK

Titles in the
Good Housekeeping Family Library
include:

Doing Up Your Home
Family Cookery
Family Health
Flower Arranging and House-Plants
Handbook of Easy Garden Plants
Home Medical Handbook
Jams and Preserves
Needlework for Pleasure
Gardening

GOOD HOUSEKEEPING FAMILY LIBRARY
MONEY-SAVING COOK BOOK

SPHERE BOOKS LIMITED
30–32 Grays Inn Road, London, WC1X 8JL

First published in Great Britain in 1974 by
Ebury Press
First Sphere Books edition 1976

ISBN 0 7221 3955 1

Edited by Gill Edden

Cover picture: Stephen Baker
Other pictures: Stephen Baker, Anthony Blake,
John Cook, Frank Coppins, Melvin Grey,
Gina Harris, Kenneth Swain, Roger Tuff
Accessories for photography:
The Kitchen Place, Guildford, Surrey; Heals, London

Printed and bound in Great Britain by
Cox & Wyman Ltd, London, Fakenham and Reading

CONTENTS

Conversion to metric measurements

The recipes in this book were not converted by rule of thumb from imperial versions, but were tested and written up using metric weights and measures, based on a 25 g unit instead of the ounce (28.35 g). Slight adjustments to this basic conversion standard were necessary in some recipes to achieve satisfactory cooking results.

If you want to convert your own recipes from imperial to metric, we suggest you use the same 25 g unit, and use 500 ml in place of 1 pint, with the British Standard 5-ml and 15-ml spoons replacing the old variable teaspoons and tablespoons; these adaptations will, however, give a slightly smaller recipe quantity and may require a shorter cooking time.

For more exact conversions and general reference, the following tables will be helpful.

Metric Conversion Scale

CAPACITY		MASS	
$\frac{1}{4}$ pint	= 142 ml	1 oz	= 28.35 g
$\frac{1}{2}$ pint	= 284 ml	2 oz	= 56.7 g
1 pint	= 568 ml	4 oz	= 113.4 g
$\frac{1}{2}$ litre	= 0.88 pints	8 oz	= 226.8 g
1 litre	= 1.76 pints	12 oz	= 340.2 g
		16 oz	= 453.6 g
		1 kilogram =	2.2 lb

LENGTH

1 in.	= 2.54 cm
6 in.	= 15.2 cm
100 cm	= 1 metre
	= 39.37 inches

Note: ml = millilitre (s); cm = centimetre (s); g = gram g

Oven Temperature Scales

° CELSIUS SCALE	ELECTRIC SCALE ° F	GAS OVEN MARKS
110 °C	225 °F	$\frac{1}{4}$
130	250	$\frac{1}{2}$
140	275	1
150	300	2
170	325	3
180	350	4
190	375	5
200	400	6
220	425	7
230	450	8
240	475	9

FOREWORD

Seafood in a cheese crust, spiced drumsticks, curried cod chowder, black cap pudding – you'll find these and many more mouth watering recipes in this book, which proves that economical eating need not be dull. Keeping the weekly budget within bounds is everyone's problem nowadays but it can be done with good planning, careful buying and clever cooking. You may not have time to experiment with recipes and won't in any case want to risk a failure. This is all the more reason for taking advantage of the Good Housekeeping Institute's tried and tested recipes. This book has been compiled by Brenda Holroyd, a former member of the Good Housekeeping Institute's staff and I am sure you will find the information she gives on buying food and planning menus a practical help towards saving money. Every recipe has been metricated. If you have any queries about them do write to us at Good Housekeeping Institute, Chestergate House, Vauxhall Bridge Road, London SW1V 1HF.

Carol Macarthur

Director
Good Housekeeping Institute

1 CUTTING THE COST

Money-saving cookery doesn't mean monotonous meals and perpetual stodge. It may mean – among other things – cheaper cuts of meat, but it also means new and interesting ways of presenting them. It means making the most of what's available at any particular time by judicious planning, preparation, and cooking.

Planning

Plan ahead – for a full week if possible – to ensure good nutritional balance and to avoid repetition, waste of left-overs and dull meals. Planning helps to economise on food, equipment and fuel costs, and it also means, of course, that you can have a once-a-week buy of most of the food although perishables must be bought more frequently. Planning means working out how much you're going to spend, and working out the meals themselves for a few days ahead, so that you can cook planned left-overs or make double batches of pastry or casseroles. Double the quantity of basic stew means two meals which, with added herbs, spices or other ingredients, will bear very little resemblance to each other when they appear on the table. Double quantity of pastry means enough for savoury *and* sweet pies and tea-time tarts. Planning also extends to the shopping and, of course, to the cooking and the time to be involved.

Shopping

Try 'own brand' products in supermarkets; many are just as good as the original brands and they are generally much cheaper. In casserole cookery, which provides no end of variety with comparatively little effort, use cheap steak where you used to use a more expensive cut and cook it more slowly. Remember that a large chicken is often a better family buy than a joint.

Lamb, pork and veal are generally cheaper than beef and just as versatile. Breast of lamb can be stuffed, rolled and served hot as a roast or cold with salad. Offal provides good nutritional value for money. But cheaper cuts of meat do tend to need more care in preparation and longer cooking time, so again it is a question of planning. Cooking a cheap cut of meat with herbs, spices and other ingredients can be unexpectedly gratifying. Money-saving

11

cookery of this kind can give you a chance to experiment successfully not only with cheaper cuts, but also with foreign dishes – as well as producing some wholesome British dishes which the family enjoy but don't have as often as they'd like.

Even at today's prices, eggs – in omelettes, soufflés, quiches and many other dishes – and cheese are good buys. They are excellent sources of protein and still relatively cheaper than meat. Pulses (i.e. peas, beans and lentils), too are high in protein but they are also high in carbohydrate, so be careful how you use them. Fish is a valuable food but as this can also be expensive it often has to be augmented with other ingredients, but if you buy herrings or whiting the food value is just the same. Canned tuna and pilchards are also comparatively cheap and tasty.

Bargain buying
Menus worked out several days ahead give you the chance, if not always to buy in bulk, at least to snap up bargains which you know you will need. That is an important point to watch; don't buy on impulse the first cut-price cans you see just because they greet you temptingly as you go into the shop. Only buy them if you can really use them. Make full use of fruit and vegetables in season too. Freezer owners can of course make even more use of them (and of bulk buys of other things) than anyone else. Make vegetables into a main dish; scallop them and serve as a supper dish with a crisp salad. If you haven't a freezer, make fruit and vegetables into jams, chutney and pickles.

Fish, home-killed meat, eggs and dairy produce all have their less expensive, if not exactly cheap, seasons. Don't overbuy, though, when it comes to packaged goods; economy sizes are all very well if you can use them before they go stale, but a waste of money otherwise.

Economy cooking
If your mother or grandmother – or you yourself – have any wartime recipe books, take a good look at them. Some of the ideas and recipes are easily adaptable for today, when prices and not simply shortage of supplies influence our purchases. Get into the habit of substituting a cheaper ingredient for a more expensive one, whenever possible. For instance, instead of buying raspberry jam for cooking try mixed fruit jam, or apple and raspberry; the colour is the same and the difference in flavour isn't all that noticeable especially if it's in a pudding to be served with custard. You can use it to fill a Swiss roll or a Victoria sponge, too. The same applies with home-made jams; your best raspberry and strawberry conserves can be kept for eating with bread and butter but jams made with cheaper fruits are excellent for cakes and puddings.

The traditional cup of tea needn't cost as much as you are currently spending on it; either cut the bill by using a lower-priced blend, or by using less of a more expensive kind, depending on your palate. Try using a little less or varying the infusion time. It is also an economy to make many more things at home; cakes, meat loaves, brawn, beefburgers are all foods that cost more, but are considerably duller, in the shop. The fuel you use for cooking will rarely even begin to make up the difference in price.

Planning your store cupboard
Keep a carefully planned store cupboard, with bay leaves, cloves, herbs and spices handy. Rice, pasta, barley, dried beans and peas are all inexpensive and satisfying if used intelligently. Cocoa and instant coffee are not there just to be drunk; use them for flavouring puddings, custards and sauces. Use instant milk powder in baking instead of fresh milk. Chill and whip evaporated milk, flavouring it with vanilla and a little icing sugar, instead of double cream for dessert toppings.

Don't throw out bread because it has gone dry; dip it in beaten milk-and-egg and fry it, then serve with melted jam or cinnamon and sugar for a delicious Poor Knights pudding. Alternatively cube the bread and fry it for croûtons for soup, or crumb it and store in airtight jars. Dry sponge or plain cake can become crumble topping for fruit pies. Soft biscuits or cornflakes can be crisped in a low oven.

Planning left-overs
Save cooking time and fuel, particularly with joints and poultry, by buying enough for two or three meals. Chop the extra pound of meat and mix it with a sharp, sweet-sour, or curry-flavoured sauce, to eat with rice or to use as a filling for pancakes. Chopped meat mixed with grated carrots and onions also provides the basis of a tasty cottage pie, or mixed with chopped potatoes, onion and herbs will make a quickly produced hash. To use up a bacon joint often an economical buy anyway), wrap slices of the cooked meat around partly boiled leeks or celery sticks, cover with cheese sauce and a sprinkling of grated cheese and brown in the oven or under the grill.

Margarine or butter?
Even if you can tell margarine from butter on your bread, the difference is not necessarily detectable in cooking, especially if the other ingredients have a more positive flavour or texture. If a recipe calls for butter you can usually quite happily substitute block margarine. Even in shortbread you can use half and half, and still get that delectable flavour. Cake tins, egg-poachers and so on can all be greased with margarine just as satisfactorily as with butter. Lard is another alternative if the buttery flavour is not important.

Bacon
Buy collar or oyster rashers, if you can get them, instead of the much more costly back or 'through' rashers. These cuts are lean and do not seem to shrink as much in cooking, while the flavour is excellent.

Blancmange
Stop buying blancmange powder; you can make it just as successfully with cornflour, with the necessary flavourings and colourings. A home-made

chocolate blancmange, made from cornflour, cocoa, sugar and milk, takes some beating!

Cream

In desserts, the smallest carton will be quite sufficient for piped rosettes for dressing up six servings. Long-life cream, rather cheaper than fresh double cream, can be whipped satisfactorily for toppings and fillings, though you may prefer to mask the 'cooked' taste with vanilla flavouring and a little sugar. Many dairies also offer whipping cream these days, which has a fat content mid-way between single and double and is cheaper than double.

Evaporated milk, too, can be chilled and treated in the same way for a topping, but don't whisk it until just before it is needed as it soon collapses. For thickening sauces and casserole dishes use single cream, not double: it does not separate as readily and the result is almost the same so far as thickening and good flavour is concerned. UHT cream can also be used here, but the final flavour tends to be rather flat. Canned creams are generally good in sauces, but do not whip well for desserts. Artificial creams in powder or liquid form are of course markedly cheaper than fresh cream but they do not have the same flavour; experiment with these and use them judiciously. In soufflés, canned cream, UHT double cream and whipping cream are all good.

So the final choice is up to you and your budget. Failing all else you can eke out cream for toppings and fillings by using 2 parts double to 1 part single, or 1 pint double and 1 tablespoon milk, or by adding an egg white before whipping if you have one left over.

Oils

Although olive oil is the classic choice for blending with vinegar as a dressing, it is not essential; in fact, for many people it is too strong and heavy. Use one of the thinner, almost flavourless oils, such as corn, sunflower or a blended type. Experiment with one or more until you find one that best suits your palate; you may need to increase the proportion of vinegar to offset the oily texture.

Vinegar

Malt or distilled vinegar, used for such things as pickles and chutneys (and fish and chips) is not everyone's choice for salad dressings. Although wine vinegar is usually used here, you can substitute 'French' vinegar – made from dried grapes instead of wine – which is cheaper, though it is more acid. Alternatively you can use cider vinegar, made from apples and pale yellow gold in colour. It is mild flavoured and less acid than wine vinegar and cheaper than French vinegar; in fact it is not much more expensive than malt vinegar.

Use vinegar as an ingredient in a marinade to give fillip and to tenderise meat before using it in a casserole.

Cooking with wine

If a recipe demands wine don't expect the same results if you replace it with anything else. You can use cider instead and get an interesting result, of course, ut it will not be 'au vin'. However, you can use a cheap wine, and if there is any left in the bottle you can keep it for several days to use in another dish. If you have no plans for using it in this way, use it to top up a bottle of wine vinegar. Rather than opening a bottle of wine specially for cooking, try replacing white wine with vermouth, if you have some handy; other commercially prepared aperitifs – which are basically fortified wines – make interesting substitutes if you want to experiment.

Meat ideas

Cook for today and tomorrow – not only stews, but a bacon joint. You can have his hot and then cold, with salad. The remains can then be chopped and the pieces used for savoury omelettes or mixed with chicken remainders in a white sauce for a suprême, or a filling for a vol-au-vent case. A piece of flank is a little on the fat side but it has many uses; in bacon and egg pie, for instance, or as a substantial spread for toast, chopped and mixed with cheese and onion. (Grill just before serving.) Cheap cuts are good, too, for quiches, minced bacon double-crust pie and baconburgers.

With a boiling fowl you can make cock-a-leekie, which gives you two courses – first broth and then meat and vegetables. When buying lamb, don't buy the breast ready stuffed or you will pay over the odds; use your own filling, or curry it, make it into a pie, or use for rissoles. Brisket, cooked slowly, makes a delicious hot roast and is just as good cold or you can use it in réchauffé dishes. Truly thrifty cooks should get back to the stockpot and make real soup. Keep a stockpot for meat trimmings and buy marrowbones. Simmer these for three hours, chill and remove the fat (you can use this for cooking). Add a few handfuls of chopped root vegetables, herbs, seasoning, and about a handful of rolled oats (for thickening) to every pint of stock, boil it gently for half an hour, and then pass it through a sieve. Reheat it when wanted, adding dumplings, macaroni or noodles for a more substantial dish.

Potatoes

Cook double the quantity of fresh potatoes and mash the remainder with milk and a little margarine before storing, covered, in the fridge, till next day. This can be used for rissoles, with left-over meat, or for a shepherd's pie; or simply heat it up by stirring, or mashing again, in a saucepan with a little additional milk, heating it gently.

2 USING YOUR EQUIPMENT

It makes money-saving sense to use all your cooking equipment – and not just your cooker – to the full. This means not using all the hot plates for vegetables and a top-of-the-stove casserole, as well as the oven for a solitary slow-cooking milk pudding. If you use the oven alone – for a casserole, pudding, baked potatoes and possibly some vegetables, too – you *will* be producing a fuel-saving meal. You will also be cooking economically if you cook vegetables and a pudding – savoury or sweet – on a single hot plate, in a steamer-and-saucepan.

A little thought beforehand can save quite a bit in fuel and still provide variety for your menus. It is sensible to cook casseroles along with not only baked or milk puddings and fruit compotes, but with slow cooking cakes, fruit breads and stewed fruit you can use later. Casseroles don't suffer from a slight lessening or increase in temperature while something else, more dependent on a constant temperature, is being cooked – providing that you adjust their cooking time accordingly. Do beware, though, of cooking a cheap cut of meat too fast in order to accommodate something else; it is easy to make it tough and hard that way.

You can use up oven space, too, by cooking a dish of savoury rice by the oven method. For two servings, allow 4 oz long grain rice, $\frac{1}{2}$ pint water and $\frac{1}{2}$ level tsp salt. Put the rice in an ovenproof casserole, add the water – boiling – with salt, and cook at 350 °F (180 °C), mark 4, for about 40 minutes. The rice will absorb the water and can be removed as soon as it is ready. Use it instead of potatoes with a savoury dish, or cool it and use it later; it can be either heated through, or used cold in a salad. (If you have a freezer, you can store it there.)

Tips to remember
It may take a little practice to organise a complete cooked meal consisting of foods that usually call for slightly different temperatures, but if you remember certain basic rules many of the difficulties disappear.
1. Make full use of the oven 'zones', remembering that when the oven is packed with food the top tends to be warmer than the bottom.

16

Make seasonal fruits into jams for the rest of the year (*see page 12*)

2. If you want something to take longer to cook than usual, put the dish in a water bath – a large meat tin or other container – containing sufficient water to reach halfway up the sides of the dish.

3. Fruit and vegetables which usually cook quickly will take longer, if you want them to, if you leave them in larger pieces than usual. Baked potatoes cook more quickly if you put a metal skewer through each of them, or prong them on one of the spikes of a gadget specially designed for the purpose. Creamed potatoes can be produced quite successfully in the oven; cook them in slices in a little milk and margarine in a covered dish, and cream them just before serving. Put frozen vegetables, unthawed, in an ovenproof dish with a little salted water and a knob of margarine; cover with foil and cook near the bottom of the oven. Empty canned vegetables into an ovenproof dish and heat through in the same way. Peel and cut up root vegetables and put these, too, in ovenproof dishes covered with foil. Cook onions and tomatoes uncovered.

Some fuel-conscious menus

Here are ideas for four menus, in which most of the dishes can be cooked in the oven simultaneously.

(Starred recipes are given later in the chapter.)

1. SHEPHERD'S PIE
   FROZEN PEAS
   TREACLE TART

Set the oven at 400 °F (200 °C), mark 6. Put the shepherd's pie on the top shelf, the tart in the middle, and the peas, unthawed, on the bottom shelf in a foil-covered ovenproof dish with a little salted water and a knob of margarine. Cook for about 30 minutes.

2. BEEF AND POTATO BRAISE*
   PLUM CRUMB BAKE*
   BAKED TOMATOES

The beef and potato braise is cooked first of all at 325 °F (170 °C), mark 3, and then at 375 °F (190 °C), mark 5. Put the tomatoes in a greased ovenproof dish, sprinkle with salt and pepper and cover with foil; put them into the oven, with the pudding, when the temperature is raised.

3. ROAST PORK (choose a joint weighing 2½–3 lb)
   ONIONS AND CARROTS
   ROAST POTATOES
   APPLE SAUCE
   RICE PUDDING

Set the oven at 400 °F (200 °C), mark 6. The pork, onions and potatoes go into a meat tin on the top shelf. Put the carrots, cut in large pieces, in a greased ovenproof dish on the middle shelf, seasoned and dotted with margarine. Put the apple sauce (slices of peeled apple dotted with a little margarine and sprinkled with a little lemon juice, in a covered ovenproof dish) and the rice pudding on the bottom shelf. Cover the rice pudding with a lid for the first hour. Cook the meat for 1 hour 30 minutes, approximately. Make the gravy from the residue in the meat tin.

4. CHICKEN CASSEROLE
ANNA POTATOES*
APPLE AND RHUBARB COBBLER*

Set the oven at 375 °F (190 °C), mark 5. Put the casserole on the top shelf, with the potatoes on the middle one and the pudding at the bottom. Cook for 40 minutes. Serve with frozen green beans, cooked alongside the pudding in the same way as the frozen peas in the first menu. Turn the potatoes out of the dish and on to a plate for serving.

As well as the traditional roast joint baked along with apple pie, you might like to try these ideas: baked chops, jacket potatoes, casserole of onions and Eve's pudding; or baked stuffed fish, creamed potatoes and queen of puddings.

Cooking meat and cakes together
Here are more ideas, based on recipes given later in the chapter, which make use of the oven for a savoury and a sweet course as well as for cakes and/or cookies. The recipes for the cakes and cookies, which are included in Chapter 10, can of course be varied; there are others equally suitable in the same chapter. The inclusion of a tea bread, or cookies which can be baked on long narrow tins, means that any space alongside a cake or small meat tin can be usefully occupied.

1. CHICKEN IN A POT*
COTTAGE PLUM UPSIDE-DOWN*
TUTTI-FRUTTI LAYER CAKE
BANANA TEA BREAD
2. POOR MAN'S MOUSSAKA*
HOT CHERRY BOMBE*
GENOESE SPONGE AND/OR MELTING MOMENTS
3. BEEF RAGOÛT*
PINEAPPLE PUDDING*
HONEY BUTTER SANDWICH
SHORTBREAD
4. ABERDEEN SAUSAGE*
APPLE MERINGUE*
ECONOMICAL CHRISTMAS CAKE

Hot plate cooking
You can use the top of the cooker economically, too. With a steamer (or two)

Pressure cookery is ideal for cheaper cuts of meat

on top of a pan of water kept continually simmering, you can cook a complete meal. A steamed savoury pudding – perhaps steak and kidney – goes in one tier or in the pan itself (stand it on an upturned saucer with the water coming halfway up the basin). Then in another tier you can have a basin of stewed apricots or prunes. Cook the vegetables round the basin. Vegetables take longer to steam than to boil, so bear this in mind; bear in mind too that as greens cook more quickly than root vegetables, these should go into the steamer, with potatoes, carrots and turnips in the bottom pan.

If you are using up the remains of a joint, heat the sliced meat in a little gravy in a shallow dish on top of the top tier, covered with a lid or foil. Or if you

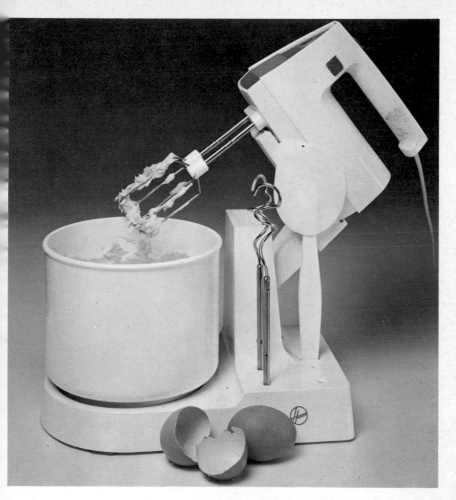

A mixer encourages you to make your own money-saving cakes

want to heat up some left-over steamed or baked pudding put that on top instead, with the vegetables and savoury pudding below.

There are other ways of using hot plates economically. If you are having sausages or beefburgers, fry them before you cook the vegetables and pudding. Keep them warm on a plate on top of the pan used for cooking the vegetables, topped with a lid or upturned basin.

Pressure cookery

A pressure cooker is a first class way of economising in cooking. It saves fuel because cooking time is so drastically reduced, and tougher and cheaper cuts of meat and boiling fowls respond well in a comparatively short time to this method. A pressure cooker is useful for making soups and stocks, cooking root vegetables, dried peas, beans and lentils and steaming puddings. It is also an asset if you do any preserving.

Blenders
A blender is not just a luxury. It will, of course, do such things as puréeing fruit and vegetables, while some models will chop them. It will blend custards and desserts, milk shakes and fresh fruit drinks, dips, sandwich fillings and pâtés. Bread and cake, fresh or stale, can be crumbed and some models will chop or grind nuts. A blender will rescue lumpy sauces, sift icing sugar, and chop hard left-over cheese – to say nothing of blending left-over vegetables for quick soups. So it can help to avoid waste – and so save money.

Slicers
A slicer enables you to make more slices of meat or vegetables than you probably could with a knife – and with far less trouble.

Electric mixers
Your electric mixer, whether a tabletop model or one held in the hand, may not be an obvious money saver, but it certainly saves time in creaming, beating, whisking and other tasks, leaving you more time for money-saving cookery elsewhere in the kitchen.

Freezers
Bulk-buys can save money, made wisely. But you can use your freezer probably more economically if you cut down on the bulk-buys of such things as grilling steaks, veal escallopes and ready-meals, and use the space for casseroles and other savoury dishes you have made yourself. It takes more time – but the family will enjoy the results and it will certainly save money. Freeze extra cakes, pies and cookies, too – made on those days when you are able to make full use of your oven by baking them along with a main meal. Freeze left-overs, too, savoury or sweet, if you have no immediate plans for a rechauffé dish making use of them; be careful not to forget these though – keeping a list of what is in store will help here.

Anna potatoes

1½ lb even-sized, waxy potatoes,   salt and pepper
   peeled (600 g)   melted margarine

Grease a thick cake tin and line the bottom with greased greaseproof paper. Trim the potatoes so that they will give equal sized slices. Slice them very thinly and arrange a layer of slightly over-lapping slices in the tin. Sprinkle with salt, pepper, and melted margarine.

Continue in this way until all the potatoes have been used, pressing each layer well into the tin. Cover with greaseproof paper and a lid and bake for about 1 hour in the centre of the oven at 375 °F (190 °C), mark 5, adding more margarine if the potatoes begin to dry. Turn out and serve at once.

Chicken in a pot

For the stuffing
4 oz sausage meat (*100 g*)
1½ oz fresh white breadcrumbs (*40 g*)
1 chicken liver, chopped
2 tbsps chopped parsley (*30 g*)

4-lb oven ready chicken (*2 kg*)
salt

freshly ground black pepper
3 oz margarine (*75 g*)
8 oz lean back bacon, in one slice (*150 g*)
1½ lb potatoes, peeled (*750 g*)
½ lb shallots, skinned (*250 g*)
1 lb small new carrots, scraped (*500 g*)
chopped parsley for garnish

(Serves 6)

Mix the stuffing ingredients. Stuff the bird at the neck end, plump up and fix with a skewer. Truss as for roasting and season well. Melt the margarine in a large pan, add the chicken and brown all over. Transfer the chicken and margarine to a large casserole. Rind the bacon and cut into ¾-in. (2-cm) cubes; add to the casserole. Cover, and cook in the oven at 350 °F (180 °C), mark 4, for 15 minutes.

Meanwhile cut the potatoes into 1-in. (2.5-cm) cubes. Remove the casserole from the oven and baste the chicken. Surround it with potatoes, shallots and carrots, turning them in the fat. Season and return the casserole to the oven and cook, covered, for a further 1½ hours until chicken and vegetables are tender. Garnish with parsley. Have a plate ready for carving the bird. Serve vegetables and juices straight from the casserole.

Aberdeen sausage

1 lb stewing beef (*400 g*)
¼ lb streaky bacon rashers,
   rinded (*100 g*)
4 oz onions, skinned (*100 g*)
4 oz rolled oats (*100 g*)

2 tsps Worcestershire sauce (*10 ml*)
1 small egg, beaten
1 level tsp salt (*5 ml*)
freshly milled black pepper
1 tbsp chopped parsley (*15 ml*)

(Serves 5–6)

Trim the meat where necessary to remove surplus fat. Put the meat, bacon and onions twice through a mincer. Add remaining ingredients and mix well. Shape into a long thick sausage and wrap in oiled foil. Fold the foil lightly across the top and twist the side edges together. Place on a baking sheet and bake at 300 °F (150 °C), mark 2 for about 2 hours. Gently remove the foil and serve hot, in thick slices.

Poor man's moussaka

(*see picture opposite*)

2 oz lard (*50 g*)
1 lb mince (*450 g*)
½ lb onions, peeled and chopped (*200 g*)
½ lb tomatoes, peeled and
   chopped (*200 g*)
   (or 6½-oz can) (*185 g approx.*)
2 tbsps chopped parsley (*30 ml*)
salt and pepper
1½ lb old potatoes, peeled and
   thinly sliced (*800 g*)

For the sauce
½ oz margarine (*15 g*)
½ oz flour (*15 g*)
½ pint milk (*300 ml*)
2 oz Cheddar cheese, grated (*50 g*)
salt and pepper
1 large egg, beaten

(Serves 5–6)

Melt the lard in a frying pan, and fry the mince until brown, stirring frequently. Add onions, tomatoes and parsley. Season well and cook for 5 minutes over a low heat. Cover the base of a 4-pint (2-litre) casserole with a layer of potato, then spoon over a layer of meat mixture. Continue, ending with a layer of potatoes. Make a cheese sauce in the usual way, with margarine, flour, milk, cheese and seasoning. Remove from the heat and beat in the egg. Pour over the potatoes. Bake the moussaka, uncovered, in the centre of the oven at 375 °F (190 °C), mark 5, for about 1 hour.

Beef and potato braise

(*see picture page 28*)

1 lb braising steak (*450 g*)
2 tbsps cooking oil (*30 ml*)
2 medium sized leeks
1½ lb potatoes, peeled (*700 g*)
salt

freshly milled black pepper
½ pint rich unseasoned beef
   stock (*300 ml*)
½ lb tomatoes, skinned (*200 g*)

(Serves 4–6)

Cut the meat into largish pieces, trimming off any excess fat. Heat the oil in a shallow frying pan and fry the meat for about 5 minutes, until evenly browned. Remove from the heat.

    Trim the leeks and cut into thin slices. Wash them well in cold water and drain. Cut the potatoes into ¼-in. (½-cm) slices. In a large shallow ovenproof casserole, 3½-pint (2-litre) capacity, add the meat and top with leeks and potatoes. Season well with salt and pepper. Pour over the beef stock and cook,

Poor man's moussaka (*opposite*)

covered, in the oven at 325 °F (170 °C), mark 3, for 1½ hours; then raise temperature to 375 °F (190 °C), mark 5, and continue to cook uncovered for 30 minutes. Brush with oil any potato surface protruding. 15 minutes before the end of cooking time tuck the tomatoes, cut into quarters, among the other vegetables.

Beef ragoût

2 lb leg of beef (*1 kg*)
2 oz seasoned flour (*50 g*)
2 tbsps cooking oil (*30 ml*)
1 large onion, skinned and sliced
1 red pepper, seeded and sliced
1 level tbsp tomato paste (*15 ml*)
1 pint beef stock (*500 ml*)
bouquet garni
salt and pepper

For the dumplings
 4 oz self-raising flour (*100 g*)
2 oz shredded suet (*50 g*)
salt
black pepper
water to mix

(Serves 5–6)

Trim the meat of any excess fat and cut into $1\frac{1}{2}$-in. (3-cm) pieces. Toss in season-ed flour. (Use plain flour if you are using a stock cube.) Heat the oil in a large pan and fry the onions and pepper gently until soft and the onions are trans-parent. Remove from the pan and put to drain on kitchen paper. Add the meat to the reheated oil in the pan; fry to seal on all sides. Lift into an ovenproof casserole, using a draining spoon, and add the vegetables. In a saucepan, blend the tomato paste with stock and bring to the boil. Pour into the casserole, add bouquet garni, adjust seasoning and cook at 300 °F (150 °C), mark 1–2, for $2\frac{1}{2}$–3 hours.

To make the dumplings, combine flour and suet, add seasoning and sufficient water to make a firm dough. Shape into 8–10 small balls. Arrange the dumplings over the ragoût. Raise the oven temperature to 375 °F (190 °C), mark 5, cover the casserole and continue to cook for a further 15 minutes.

Plum crumb bake

2 oz margarine (*50 g*)
4 oz fresh white breadcrumbs (*100 g*)
$\frac{1}{4}$ level tsp ground cinnamon (*1.25 ml*)
1 oz Demerara sugar (*25 g*)

1 lb plums (or 2×1-lb 13-oz cans)
 (*450 g or 2×822-g cans*)
3 tbsps golden syrup (for fresh plums) (*45 ml*)

(Serves 4)

Melt the margarine in a frying pan, add the crumbs in a shallow layer and cook, turning often, until beginning to colour. Combine the cinnamon and sugar and stir into the golden crumbs. Meanwhile, halve the plums, remove the stones and place the fruit in a 2-pint (1-litre) pie dish. Spoon the golden syrup over; if using canned plums, drain off the syrup, reduce it to a glaze by fast boiling and use this instead of golden syrup. Cook, uncovered, in the oven, at 375 °F (190 °C), mark 5, for about 20 minutes (5 minutes if using canned fruit). Spoon the crumbs over and continue to cook for another 15 minutes. Serve warm with pouring custard.

Apple and rhubarb cobbler
(see picture page 29)

1-lb 3-oz can rhubarb (or, better still, your own bottled rhubarb) (*about 538 g*)
$1\frac{1}{2}$ lb cooking apples, peeled and cored (*700 g*)
4 oz caster sugar (*100 g*)

1 oz stem ginger, chopped (*25 g*)
4 oz margarine (*100 g*)
vanilla essence
1 egg yolk
5 oz self-raising flour (*125 g*)
crushed cornflakes

(Serves 6)

Drain the rhubarb and measure off $\frac{1}{4}$ pint (150 ml) syrup. Thickly slice the apples into a saucepan; sprinkle over 1 oz (25 g) caster sugar and the measured syrup. Bring to the boil, then simmer gently until tender – about 20 minutes. Combine the fruit and ginger and pour it into a 2-pint (1-litre) ovenproof pie dish.

Cream the margarine and remaining sugar together until soft and fluffy. Beat in a few drops vanilla essence and the egg yolk. Gradually stir in the flour and mix to a smooth dough. With wet hands, shape mixture into 20–24 small balls. Roll them in cornflakes and arrange over the fruit. Bake at 375 °F (190 °C), mark 5, for about 30 minutes until golden brown. Serve with pouring custard.

Pineapple pudding
(see picture page 32)

2 oz margarine (*50 g*)
4 oz caster sugar (*100 g*)
2 eggs, separated
1 oz plain flour (*25 g*)

8-oz can pineapple rings (*226 g*)
$\frac{3}{4}$ pint milk, approx. (*400 ml*)
cherries and angelica to decorate (optional)

(Serves 4)

Cream the margarine and 2 oz (50g) sugar until light and fluffy. Beat in the egg yolks and flour. Drain the pineapple and measure the juice; make up to $\frac{3}{4}$ pint (400ml) with the milk. Heat the milk and juice, but do not boil. Gradually pour on to the creamed mixture. Return to the pan and cook until thick and creamy without boiling, stirring all the time. Pour the custard into a 2-pint (1-litre) capacity ovenproof dish. Arrange four pineapple rings on top of the custard.

Whisk the egg whites until stiff. Add $1\frac{1}{2}$ oz (40g) sugar and whisk again until stiff. With a large star nozzle, pipe the meringue in four whirls on top of the pineapple rings. Sprinkle with the remaining sugar. Cook in the oven at 300 °F (150 °C), mark 2, for about 30 minutes, until the meringue is pale golden in colour. Decorate with cherries and angelica if wished.

Beef and potato braise (*page 24*)

Apple meringue

6-oz jam Swiss roll (*170 g*)
grated rind and juice of 1 lemon or orange
¾ pint thick apple purée (from 4 cooking apples, about 6 oz each) (*150 g each*)

2 egg whites
4 oz caster sugar (*100 g*)

(Serves 4)

Slice the Swiss roll and arrange in the base of a 2-pint (1-litre) soufflé dish. Spoon over the grated rind and juice. Spread the apple over the sponge. Whisk the egg whites until stiff; whisk in 2 oz (50g) sugar until the meringue stiffens again, then fold in all but 1 level tbsp (15 ml) of the remaining sugar.

28

Apple and rhubarb cobbler (*page 27*)

Pile over the apple, pull up in peaks and dredge with the remaining sugar. Cook in the oven at 300 °F (150 °C), mark 2, for about 30 minutes. Serve warm. If preferred, trifle sponge cake can be used instead of jam roll; sandwich it with jam.

Cottage plum upside-down

1 can (about 1 lb 4 oz) golden plums
  (about 566 g)
2 tbsps golden syrup (30 ml)
3 oz margarine (75 g)
3 oz sugar (75 g)
1 large egg

5 oz self-raising flour (125 g)
½ level tsp ground ginger (2.5 ml)
1–2 tbsps milk (15–30 ml)
3 level tsps arrowroot (15 ml)
knob of margarine or butter

(Serves 4)

Drain the juice from the plums and reserve. Arrange the plums in a buttered 2-pint (1-litre) pie dish and drizzle the syrup over them. Cream the margarine and sugar thoroughly and beat in egg. Lightly beat in the sifted flour and ginger with milk to give a stiff dropping consistency. Cover the plums with this sponge mixture. Place the dish on a baking sheet and bake at 350 °F (180 °C), mark 4, for about 45 minutes.

To serve, have ready the juice thickened with arrowroot and a knob of margarine or butter added. Turn the pudding upside down on to a hot plate and serve the thickened juice separately.

Hot cherry bombe

8 oz self-raising flour (200 g)
pinch of salt
4 oz butter or margarine (100 g)
4 oz caster sugar (100 g)
few drops of vanilla essence

1 egg, beaten
14¼-oz can cherry pie filling
  (about 400 g)
1 oz Demerara sugar (25 g)
1 oz flaked almonds (25 g)

(Serves 4)

Sift together the flour and salt. Rub in the butter. Stir in the sugar, vanilla essence and beaten egg, and mix to a soft but manageable dough. Line a buttered ovenproof 2-pint (1-litre) pudding basin with two-thirds of the dough. (Press the mixture against the base and sides, using a round-bladed knife; ensure that the surface is completely covered.) Pour the pie filling into the centre. Roll out the remaining pastry and use it to cover the top of the basin. Press down the edges well to seal. Bake in the oven at 375 °F (190 °C), mark 5, for about 1 hour, until crisp and golden then unmould on to a warm serving plate. Mix together the Demerara sugar and almonds and sprinkle over the top of the pudding. Serve with thick pouring cream or a sweet white sauce.

3 MAKING FOOD STRETCH

Anyone can make a little go a long way by heaping mashed potatoes on a bit of minced meat and calling it shepherd's pie, or by putting slices of ham between slices of bread and simply having a sandwich. But there's a world of difference between that and judiciously blending several ingredients to make a complete and satisfying meal. Use rice and pasta to eke out small quantities of meat, poultry and fish in pilaus, risottos and other 'foreign' dishes. (Don't buy the canned, made-up sort, they work out expensive.) Use pearl barley and lentils for giving body to soups. Rice, tapioca and semolina make delicious desserts in pretty moulds, or baked in the traditional way and served with top of the milk, jam or sauce.

Remember there are lots of possible fillings for quiches, providing you have the eggs for the custard. As a change from bacon, onion and cheese, try these fillings: bacon and sweet corn; smoked haddock and cheese (see photograph on page 37); tuna, cheese and onion.

Meat pie or a steak and kidney pudding will be more filling and will go further than meat or steak and kidney would on their own. The same applies to a meat loaf in a pastry case. Stretch stews and casseroles with dumplings, plain or herb flavoured, or give them a cobbler topping with rounds of a plain (or herby) scone mixture.

Mince left-over meat or fish and mix with mashed potatoes for rissoles or fish cakes; or incorporate – sliced or chopped – in a thick batter for fritters. Add finely chopped left-over meat or fish to scrambled eggs, for a lunch or supper-time snack with a difference.

Chicken bake

6 oz cooked chicken, diced (150 g)
2 oz margarine (50 g)
2 medium onions, skinned and chopped
3 sticks celery, chopped
2 oz peanuts (50 g)

2 level tbsps flour (30 ml)
½ pint milk (250 ml)
2–3 oz tasty Cheddar, grated (50–70 g)
small packet crisps, crushed

(Serves 4)

Pineapple pudding (*page 27*)

Place the chicken in a small casserole or pie dish. Melt the margarine and sauté the onion until transparent, then add the celery and peanuts and fry gently for 2–3 minutes. Sprinkle the flour into the pan; blend and cook for 1–2 minutes. Gradually stir in the milk and cook, stirring, until thick and smooth. Add half the cheese and stir to blend; pour over the chicken. Mix together the remaining cheese with the crushed crisps and sprinkle over the top. Bake at 400 °F (200 °C), mark 6, for about 30 minutes until crisp and golden. Serve with a tomato and cucumber salad.

Beef and potato charlotte

2 lb potatoes, peeled and thinly
  sliced (1 kg)
6 oz onion, skinned and chopped (150 g)
1 oz margarine (25 g)
½ lb minced beef (200 g)
½ lb belly of pork, minced (200 g)
3 tomatoes, skinned and sliced

2 oz fresh white breadcrumbs (50 g)
2 level tbsps tomato paste (30 ml)
good pinch mixed herbs
salt and pepper
1 egg, beaten
2 oz cheese, grated (50 g)

(Serves 4–5)

Cook the potatoes in boiling salted water for 2 minutes. Drain and set aside to cool. Sauté the onion in the margarine, combine it with the rest of the ingredients, except the egg and cheese. Grease an 8½-in. (22-cm) spring-release tin with a plain base and stand it on a baking tray. Arrange potatoes, overlapping, in the base and around the sides. Brush with egg. Pack in half the meat, top with more potato, the rest of the meat and finally potato. Press down well, sprinkle with cheese and bake at 425 °F (220 °C), mark 7, for about 1¼ hours. Remove the tin, brush potatoes with more beaten egg and cook for a further 15 minutes or until golden.

Leek and bacon pilaff

1 lb lean streaky bacon rashers, rinded
  (450 g)
2 lb leeks (1 kg)
2 oz margarine (50 g)
4 oz onion, skinned and chopped (100 g)

6 oz American long grain rice (150 g)
1 pint stock (500 ml)
salt and freshly ground black pepper

(Serves 4)

Dice the bacon and fry until the fat begins to run. Trim the leeks, discarding about two-thirds of the green part (this can be used for soup). Slice the leeks and wash in plenty of cold water. Drain. Add to the bacon and sauté for 5 minutes. Remove from pan, drain, and put to one side. Melt the margarine and sauté the onion until soft. Add the rice and fry for a further 3 minutes.

Pour stock into the pan, bring to the boil and cook, covered, for about 10 minutes. Add the leek and bacon mixture and cook for a further 10 minutes or until the leeks are tender. Season and serve with a bowl of grated cheese.

Liver risotto

1½ oz lard (*40 g*)
1 lb lamb's liver, cut in ¼-in. cubes (*450 g; ½-cm cubes*)
2 medium onions, skinned and chopped
2 sticks celery, chopped
2 large tomatoes, skinned, seeded and diced

6 oz long grain rice (*150 g*)
1 pint stock, made with a cube (*550 ml*)
3 level tbsps tomato paste (*45 ml*)
salt and pepper

(Serves 4–6)

Melt half the fat in a flameproof casserole and fry the liver quickly until just brown. Remove from the casserole, melt the remaining fat and fry the onion and celery over a low heat until tender. Replace the liver and add the tomatoes, rice, stock and tomato paste. Season well, cover, and cook in the oven at 350 °F (180 °C), mark 4, for about 1 hour or until the rice is cooked and most of the liquid is absorbed.

Cheese and beef roly poly

For suet crust
8 oz self-raising flour (*200 g*)
4 oz shredded suet (*100 g*)
4 oz Cheddar cheese, finely grated (*100 g*)
pinch of salt
cold water to mix

For filling
1 lb beef, minced (*450 g*)
4 oz onion, skinned and finely chopped (*100 g*)
1 level tsp dried marjoram (*5 ml*)
1 oz fresh white breadcrumbs (*25 g*)
salt and pepper
1 egg, beaten

(Serves 4–6)

Mix in a bowl the flour, suet, cheese and salt. Add enough cold water to mix to a soft elastic dough. Knead lightly on a floured board and roll into a rectangle 12 in. by 10 in. (30 cm by 25 cm). In a bowl mix together the beef, onion, marjoram, breadcrumbs, salt and pepper. Add the egg and mix well. Spread the meat mixture over the rectangle of pastry to within 1 in. (2 cm) of one long edge and brush the remaining strip with water. Carefully roll up and wrap loosely in oiled aluminium foil. Seal the ends well.

Place the roly poly in a roasting tin in ¼ in. (½ cm) of water. Bake in the centre of the oven at 325 °F (170 °C), mark 3, for 2 hours. Serve hot.

Veal and vegetable pie

2–3 tbsps cooking oil (*30–45 ml*)
4 oz celery, finely chopped (*100 g*)
1 lb pie veal, minced (*500 g*)
2 oz fresh white breadcrumbs (*50 g*)
salt and pepper
1 egg, beaten
1 oz flour (*25 g*)

1 lb leeks, washed (*500 g*)
½ pint chicken stock, made with a
  cube (*250 ml*)
8 oz shortcrust pastry
  (8 oz flour, etc) (*200 g*)
milk

(Serves 5–6)

Heat half the oil and fry the celery for 5 minutes. Mix together the celery, veal, breadcrumbs, salt, pepper and egg. Form into 16 balls and toss them in flour. Heat the remaining oil, add the balls and fry gently for 10 minutes. Drain.

Slice the leeks finely and place them in a 2½-pint (2-litre) oval pie dish. Put the meatballs on top, add stock and seasoning. Cover the pie dish with pastry, brush with milk, then make a slit in the centre. Bake in the centre of the oven at 400 °F (200 °C), mark 6, for 20 minutes. Reduce heat to 350 °F (180 °C), mark 4, and cook for a further 40 minutes.

Cannelloni au gratin

12 cannelloni
1 tbsp cooking oil (*15 ml*)
4 oz streaky bacon, rinded and
  finely chopped (*100 g*)
1 lb minced steak (*400 g*)
4 oz onion, skinned and finely
  sliced (*100 g*)
2¼-oz can tomato paste (*63 g*)
½ level tsp dried *fines herbes* (*2.5 ml*)

For the sauce
1½ oz butter (*40 g*)
1 oz flour (*25 g*)
¾ pint milk (*400 ml*)
4 oz mature Cheddar cheese,
  grated (*100 g*)
salt and pepper
nutmeg and cayenne pepper

(Serves 4–6)

Cook the cannelloni as directed on the packet; cool under running water and drain carefully. In a frying pan, heat the oil and fry the bacon until crisp. Add the minced steak and onion and fry until the meat is fully cooked. Drain off any surplus fat before stirring in the tomato paste and herbs. Using a teaspoon, and standing the cooked cannelloni up on end, carefully fill each one with meat. Lay horizontally in a buttered ovenproof dish.

In a saucepan, melt the butter and stir in the flour. Cook the roux for 1–2 minutes. Off the heat, gradually stir in the milk. Bring to the boil and cook for 2–3 minutes, until thickened. Stir in the cheese. Season with salt and pepper and pour over the cannelloni. Lightly sprinkle with spices and bake

Smoked haddock and cheese quiche (*page 33*)

in the oven at 400 °F (200 °C), mark 6, for about 30 minutes, until bubbling and golden brown.

Toad in the hole

4 oz plain flour (*100 g*)
½ level tsp salt (*2.5 ml*)
1 egg

½ pint milk and water, mixed (*250 ml*)
1 lb skinless sausages (*450 g*)

(Serves 4)

Put the flour and salt into a bowl. Add egg and half the liquid. Gradually stir in the flour and beat until smooth. Stir in the remaining liquid. Grease a shallow ovenproof dish or Yorkshire pudding tin, put in the sausages and pour in the batter. Bake at the top of the oven for 40–45 minutes at 425 °F (220 °C), mark 7, or until the batter is well risen and golden brown.

Kedgeree

8 oz long grain rice (*200 g*)
1½ lb smoked haddock fillet (*800 g*)
2 oz margarine (*50 g*)
2 oz butter (*50 g*)
½ level tsp cayenne pepper (*2.5 ml*)

4 eggs, hardboiled
salt
freshly milled black pepper
chopped parsley

(Serves 4–6)

Cook the rice in boiling salted water until tender. Drain in a colander. Place the haddock in a shallow pan, cover with cold water. Bring to the boil, then reduce the heat to low and simmer uncovered for about 10 minutes. Drain the fish and place it on a plate; break up, with a fork, into large flakes and discard the skin and bones. Cover and set aside.

Melt the butter and margarine in a heavy-based pan, sprinkle with cayenne pepper and cook over a low heat, stirring constantly, for about 1 minute. Stir the rice into the fat, add fish and return the saucepan to low heat. Toss the rice and fish together gently; cook for 1–2 minutes until reheated. Add the egg whites, chopped finely. Season to taste and transfer to a deep heated platter. Garnish with sieved egg yolk and chopped parsley, arranged in lines. Serve at once.

Cold beef salad

8 oz long grain rice (*200 g*)
2–3 tomatoes, skinned and sliced
8 oz cold cooked beef, thinly sliced (*300 g*)

1 small onion, skinned and finely chopped
1 tsp made mustard (*5 ml*)
3 tbsps French dressing (*45 ml*)

(Serves 4–6)

Cook the rice in boiling salted water, drain and allow it to cool. Mix it with the tomatoes, meat and onion. Add the mustard to the French dressing, and stir into the salad ingredients.

Dressed sausage and potato

¾ lb new potatoes (*400 g*)
7 tbsps French dressing (*100 ml*)
1 egg, hard boiled
½ lb sausages, cooked and
  cooled (*200 g*)

4 sticks celery, finely sliced
4 spring onions, scissor snipped
1 tbsp chopped parsley (*15 ml*)

(Serves 4)

Boil the potatoes, drain well and slice roughly while still hot. Spoon over half the French dressing. Leave to cool. Cut the sausages into thin slices and add the celery.

Arrange the potatoes carefully in a serving dish. Chop the egg finely, add the spring onions, the parsley, sausages and celery. Toss in the remainder of the dressing and spoon the salad over the potatoes. Leave in a cool place – but not the refrigerator – for ½ hour. Serve with crisp lettuce.

Curried rice salad

8 oz long grain rice (*200 g*)
8 level tbsps thick mayonnaise (*100 ml*)
1–2 level tsps curry paste (*5–10 ml*)
little grated orange rind
black pepper

4 rings canned pineapple
8 oz sliced cooked ham or cooked
  white chicken meat (*200 g*)
chopped parsley

(Serves 4–6)

Cook the rice in boiling salted water until tender. Drain in a sieve and, to cool quickly, run cold water over. Drain again. In a bowl, combine the mayonnaise, curry paste, orange rind and freshly milled black pepper to taste. With a sharp knife or scissors, cut the pineapple into thin pieces and fold into half the mayonnaise with the cool rice. Arrange the rice in a bed on a flat dish. With scissors, cut the ham or chicken into fingers and fold through the remaining mayonnaise. Pile on to the rice and garnish with chopped parsley.

4 SUSTAINING SOUPS

Don't regard soups just as quick snacks or starters; make them into hearty, sustaining family meals. Serve these super-soups with rolls (preferably heated in the oven, or – fuel-saving, this – on a plate on top of the saucepan as the soup simmers) or with French bread. Follow with cheese and/or fruit for a wholesome, tasty meal. Soups like this can be prepared in advance, ready to be heated and any finishing touches added when you come in after a day in the country or a morning in town.

If you are using canned soup, try to add something extra to boost the flavouring or texture – home-made stock, cooked vegetables, extra herbs or croûtons, for instance. Even another can – such as tomatoes or mixed vegetables or chopped chicken – can make quite a difference.

Cream of artichoke soup
(*see picture opposite*)

2 lb Jerusalem artichokes (*1 kg*)
2 slices of lemon
1½ pints water (*750 ml*)
1 oz butter or margarine (*25 g*)
4 oz onions, skinned and
    chopped (*100 g*)
2 level tbsps cornflour (*30 ml*)
¾ pint milk (*400 ml*)

1½ tbsps lemon juice (*20 ml*)
2 level tbsps chopped parsley (*30 ml*)
1½ level tsps salt (*7 ml*)
white pepper
2½ fl oz single cream or top of the
    milk (*60 ml*)
croûtons

(Makes 2¼ pints) (*1.2 litres*)

Wash the artichokes well. Place them in a large saucepan with the lemon slices, cover with water, bring to the boil and cook until tender – about 20 minutes. Drain off the water and reserve 1 pint. Allow the artichokes to cool before peeling away the skins. Mash roughly.

Melt the butter or margarine in a clean saucepan, add the onion and fry until soft but not coloured. Stir in the cornflour, reserved artichoke water and

40

milk, then stir in the artichokes. Bring the sauce to the boil, stirring. Cook for 2–3 minutes, then remove from the heat and purée in an electric blender. Return it to the saucepan, stir in the lemon juice, parsley, seasoning and cream or top of the milk. Bring to serving temperature and garnish with croûtons.

Potato and leek soup
(*see picture page 44*)

12 oz leeks (*300 g*)
1 oz butter or margarine (*25 g*)
1½ lb potatoes (*750 g*)
3 pints light stock (*1.5 litres*)
bouquet garni

salt and freshly ground black pepper
French bread
grated cheese
chopped parsley

(Makes 3¾ pints) (*about 2 litres*)

Discard a third of the green top from the leeks; slice the remainder finely and wash thoroughly. Drain and place in a large saucepan with the butter or margarine; cover and sauté for 5 minutes.

Meanwhile, peel and roughly dice the potatoes and add to the pan with the stock, bouquet garni and seasoning. Bring to the boil, reduce heat, cover, and simmer for about 1 hour until the potatoes are soft. Discard the bouquet garni. Purée in an electric blender or pass through a sieve. Return the soup to the pan, thin if necessary with a little extra stock (¼ pint or 150 ml), adjust the seasoning and serve with slices of French bread topped with grated cheese and grilled. Garnish the soup with chopped parsley.

Golden vegetable soup

6 oz potatoes (*150 g*)
6 oz turnips (*150 g*)
6 oz carrots (*150 g*)
6 oz onions (*150 g*)
6 oz celery (*150 g*)
1½ pints unseasoned bone or chicken
  stock (*750 ml*)

salt and freshly ground black pepper
bouquet garni
1 oz butter or margarine (*25 g*)
Parmesan cheese
celery leaves for garnish

(Makes 1¾ pints) (*1 litre*)

Peel the potatoes, turnips and carrots. Skin the onions and chop finely. Slice the celery finely. Grate the potatoes, turnips and carrots into a large pan; add the onion, celery and stock together with 1 level tsp (5 ml) salt, a little pepper and a bouquet garni. Bring to the boil, reduce the heat, cover and simmer for about 1 hour. Adjust seasoning, add the butter or margarine and when melted serve the soup with a dusting of grated Parmesan cheese and snipped celery leaves.

Curried cod chowder

1½ lb cod fillet (or other white fish) (750 g)
1½ pints water (800 ml)
salt and freshly ground black pepper
8 oz potatoes, peeled (200 g)
2 oz butter (50 g)
6 oz onions, skinned and chopped (150 g)

6 oz celery, trimmed and chopped (150 g)
½ level tsp mild curry powder (2.5 ml)
3 level tbsps flour (45 ml)
½ pint creamy milk (250 ml)
chopped parsley and chives

(Makes 3½ pints) (about 1.5 litres)

Wipe the fish with a damp cloth. Place it in a large saucepan, pour over the cold water and season. Bring nearly to the boil, then remove from the heat and skim off the surface froth. Carefully lift out the fish, using a draining spoon, and put it on a plate. Remove the skin and bones, flake it into bite-size portions and leave to one side. Strain and reserve the fish stock. Cut the potatoes into small dice. Bring them to the boil in salted water; cook until tender, then drain and reserve. Melt the butter in a large flameproof casserole. Stir in the onions and celery and cook slowly until soft but not brown. Stir the curry powder and flour into the vegetables, then gradually blend in the fish stock and milk. Bring to the boil, cook for 2–3 minutes then reduce the heat to simmering before adding the potatoes and fish; adjust seasoning. Garnish with chopped parsley and chives and serve with warm French bread.

Minestrone à la milanese

12 oz potatoes, peeled (300 g)
8 oz cabbage heart, shredded (200 g)
4 oz celery (100 g)
6 oz onions, skinned (150 g)
3 tomatoes, skinned and quartered
4 tbsps cooking oil (60 ml)
2 oz green streaky bacon, rinded and finely diced (50 g)

3 pints white stock (1.5 litres)
1 clove garlic, skinned and crushed
¼ lb ham in one piece, diced (100 g)
salt and freshly ground black pepper
bouquet garni
2 oz frozen peas (50 g)
1½ oz Parmesan cheese, grated (40 g)
chopped parsley

(Makes 4 pints) (2 litres)

Prepare all the vegetables; cut the potatoes, celery and onions into small dice. Heat the oil and fry the bacon until cooked but not brown; add the prepared vegetables and cook for 5 minutes more, stirring frequently. Drain

43

Potato and leek soup (*page 42*) Cream of carrot and lettuce soup (*opposite*)

and place in a large flameproof casserole or saucepan. Pour over the stock and add the garlic, ham, seasoning and bouquet garni. Simmer, covered, for 2 hours.

Add the peas and cheese and cook for 10 minutes longer. Garnish with lots of chopped parsley.

Oxtail with mustard dumplings

(*see picture opposite*)

1 oxtail (2 lb) chopped into small
  pieces (*1 kg*)
2 tbsps cooking oil (*30 ml*)
4 oz celery, trimmed and diced (*100 g*)
4 oz carrots, peeled and diced (*100 g*)
1 small turnip, peeled and diced
3 pints rich beef stock (*1.5 litres*)
1 level tsp salt (*5 ml*)
freshly ground black pepper
bouquet garni
½ tsp gravy browning (*2.5 ml*)
¾ level tsp concentrated curry
  sauce (*5 ml*)
½–¾ pint beef stock (*250–300 ml*)

For the dumplings
3 oz self-raising flour (*75 g*)
¾ level tsp dry mustard (*5 ml*)
1½ oz shredded suet (*40 g*)
½ level tsp salt (*2.5 ml*)
freshly ground black pepper
water

(Makes about 3 pints) (*1.5 litres*)

Wipe the oxtail with a damp cloth and remove any excess fat. Place the meat in a frying pan with the oil and fry briskly to seal. Drain and place in a large saucepan. Fry the vegetables in the reheated meat residue for 3–4 minutes.

44

Add to the meat. Pour the stock over, season well, add the bouquet garni, then cover and simmer for 4 hours.

Strain the soup and discard the bouquet garni. Chill the meat juices to allow the fat to set; remove the fat and take all the flesh from the bones. Reheat the oxtail juices and vegetables and purée them in an electric blender. Return to pan and stir in last three ingredients – gravy browning, concentrated curry sauce and stock. Bring to the boil, reduce the heat, check seasoning and add the dumplings. Cook for about 30 minutes more.

To make the dumplings: Sift the flour and mustard together, then stir in the suet, salt and pepper. Add water to mix to give a firm dough. Shape into about 20 small balls.

Cream of carrot and lettuce soup
(see picture opposite)

1½ lb carrots (750 g)
1½ pints veal bone stock (800 ml)
salt and freshly ground black pepper
2 oz bacon rashers, rinded (50 g)

1 oz butter or margarine (25 g)
1 small lettuce
½ pint veal bone stock (250 ml)
1 oz vermicelli (25 g)

(Makes 2 pints) (1 litre)

Oxtail makes a rich, sustaining soup

Pare the carrots and slice them thickly. Place in a large saucepan with the stock and seasoning. Bring to the boil, reduce heat, cover and simmer until the carrots are tender – about 45 minutes. Purée in an electric blender.

Meanwhile, snip the bacon into very small dice, using kitchen scissors. In the clean pan, melt the butter or margarine, add the bacon and fry slowly until the bacon is lightly browned. Trim the lettuce and chop with a stainless steel knife; add it to the pan, stir and add the puréed carrot and ½ pint (250 ml) stock. Sprinkle in the vermicelli, bring to the boil, adjust seasoning and cook a further 10 minutes.

Thick pea and ham potage

4 oz split green peas, soaked
   overnight (100 g)
salt
2 oz butter or margarine (50 g)
6 oz celery, trimmed and sliced (150 g)
6 oz potatoes, peeled and
   sliced (150 g)
2 oz onions, skinned and diced (50 g)

6 oz leeks, trimmed and finely
   sliced (150 g)
1 tbsp chopped parsley (15 ml)
1 level tbsp flour (15 ml)
2 pints chicken stock (1 litre)
freshly ground black pepper
¼–½ lb cooked ham, diced (100–200 g)
chopped parsley

(Makes 3 pints) (1.5 litres)

Cover the soaked peas with water, to which ¼ level tsp (1.25 ml) salt has been added. Bring to the boil; boil for 2–3 minutes. Reduce the heat, cover, and cook for about 1 hour until soft.

Melt the butter in a saucepan and add the celery, potato, onion, well washed leeks and parsley. Cook, covered, until the vegetables are tender but not coloured. Stir in the flour and cook for 1–2 minutes. Gradually blend in the stock, 2 level tsps salt (10 ml) and a little pepper. Bring to the boil, reduce heat, cover and simmer for 30 minutes. Drain the peas; add them to other vegetables and stir through. Purée in an electric blender in convenient amounts. Reheat the soup with the ham to serving temperature. Garnish with parsley.

Note: Omit the white soaking tablet generally supplied with peas.

Minted lamb broth

1 lb onions, skinned (400 g)
2 oz butter or margarine (50 g)
1 lb breast of lamb, chopped (400 g)
2 level tsps salt (10 ml)
½ level tsp pepper (2.5 ml)

water
1 oz vermicelli (25 g)
2 tomatoes
2 tsps freshly chopped mint (10 ml)

(Makes 3 pints) (about 1.5 litres)

Halve the onions lengthwise and slice very finely. Melt the butter in a large pan and slowly fry the onion until golden. Cut the lamb through into pieces and add to the pan with the salt, pepper, and 2 pints (1 litre) water. Bring to the boil, reduce the heat, cover and simmer for about 1 hour, until the meat comes away from the bones.

Remove the meat from the liquor; discard the bones and any skin and tough tissue. Chop the meat and return it to the pan with an extra ½ pint (250 ml) water and the vermicelli. Skin and seed the tomatoes and dice the flesh; add to the pan with the mint and simmer for a further 10 minutes. Adjust seasoning before serving in large bowls with hot French bread.

Easy tomato soup

4 oz onions, skinned (100 g)
3 cloves
2-lb 3-oz can tomatoes (about 990 g)
sprig parsley
1 bayleaf
1 level tsp salt (5 ml)
freshly ground black pepper
¼ level tsp freshly grated
   nutmeg (1.25 ml)

2 oz butter (50 g)
3 level tbsps flour (45 ml)
¾ pint milk (400 ml)
¼ pint light stock (150 ml)
2–3 tbsps single cream or top of the
   milk (30–45 ml)

(Makes 2 pints) (about 1 litre)

Cut onion into small chunks and stud one piece with cloves. Place the onions, tomatoes (with juice), sprig of parsley, bayleaf, seasoning and nutmeg in a saucepan. Bring to the boil, reduce heat, cover and simmer for 1 hour.

Melt the butter in a second pan and blend in the flour. Cook the roux for 2–3 minutes before gradually stirring in the milk to give a smooth paste. Bring to the boil, stirring; reduce heat and simmer for 5 minutes.

Remove the bayleaf, cloves and parsley from the tomato mixture. Purée it in an electric blender and pass through a fine sieve to remove pips. Add to the white sauce, blend them well together with a spoon or in the blender. Stir in the stock and cream; adjust seasoning and reheat to serving temperature, but do not boil. Just before serving, whirl some cream over the surface.

French onion soup
(see picture overleaf)

8 oz onions, skinned (200 g)
1 oz butter (25 g)
1 oz flour (25 g)
1½ pints rich brown stock (800 ml)
1 bayleaf

1 level tsp salt (5 ml)
freshly ground black pepper
2 oz French bread (50 g)
1–2 oz Cheddar or Parmesan cheese,
   grated (25–50 g)

(Makes about 1½ pints) (about 1 litre)

French onion soup

Cut the onions into quarters and then into thin slices. Melt the butter in a saucepan. Fry the onion for 5–10 minutes until well browned then stir in the flour and cook for 2 minutes, stirring frequently. Pour in the stock and season with bayleaf, salt and pepper. Stir over the heat until the soup boils, then reduce heat and simmer for 10 minutes. Remove the bayleaf. Cut the bread into thin slices and cover with grated cheese. Pour the soup into a flame-proof casserole and arrange the bread on top. Place in a hot oven or under the grill until the cheese is melted and bubbling. Serve at once.

Note: When a rather light stock is used, add a little gravy browning.

Chunky courgette soup

(*see picture opposite*)

4 oz haricot beans (*100 g*)
salt
12 oz potatoes (*300 g*)
8 oz courgettes, trimmed (*200 g*)
12 oz leeks, washed (*300 g*)
1 clove garlic, crushed
2 tbsps cooking oil (*30 ml*)

2 oz butter (*50 g*)
2 pints chicken or veal stock (*1 litre*)
freshly ground black pepper
½ level tsp dried basil (*2.5 ml*)
4 oz Cheddar cheese, grated (*100 g*)
chopped parsley

(Makes about 3½ pints) (*about 2 litres*)

Soak the beans overnight in water, then drain. Put the soaked beans in a sauce-pan, cover with salted fresh water and simmer, covered, for 1½ hours. Drain. Peel and dice the potatoes; slice the courgettes into chunky slices, about ¼ in.

Chunky courgette soup

($\frac{1}{2}$ cm) thick. Combine the leek with the garlic. Heat the oil; fry the potato first for 2–3 minutes, then drain, using a slotted spoon. Place in a large saucepan. Sauté the leeks for about 5 minutes, stirring frequently, then drain and add to the potato. Lastly melt the butter, add the courgettes and cook for about 5 minutes. Add to pan with the beans. Pour over the stock; add seasoning and basil. Cover and simmer for 1$\frac{1}{4}$ hours until the vegetables are tender. Sprinkle cheese over the soup during the last 15 minutes of cooking. Check the seasoning and garnish with chopped parsley.

Canadian cheese soup

$\frac{1}{2}$ lb potatoes, peeled (200 g)
$\frac{1}{2}$ lb onions, skinned (200 g)
2 oz carrots, pared (50 g)
2 oz celery, trimmed and diced (50 g)
$\frac{1}{2}$ pint water (250 ml)
1 pint rich turkey or chicken
   stock (500 ml)

$\frac{1}{4}$ lb mature Cheddar cheese,
   grated (100 g)
3 tbsps single cream or top of the
   milk (45 ml)
salt and pepper
2 tbsps chopped parsley (30 ml)

(Makes about 2$\frac{1}{2}$ pints) (about 1 litre)

Finely slice or dice the potatoes, onions and carrots. Place in a saucepan with the celery and water. Bring to the boil, reduce heat, cover and simmer for about 20 minutes, until the vegetables are tender. Add the rest of the ingredients, except the parsley, and reheat without boiling. Adjust seasoning, sprinkle in the parsley and serve.

Lentil soup

4 oz lentils (100 g)
3 pints stock (1.5 litres)
2 onions, skinned and chopped
3 carrots, peeled and diced
1 turnip, peeled and grated

4 sticks celery, trimmed and chopped
bouquet garni
salt and pepper
chopped parsley

(Serves 4)

Pour boiling water over the lentils and leave to soak for 2–3 hours. Bring the stock to the boil, add the drained lentils, prepared vegetables and seasonings. Simmer gently for 1$\frac{1}{2}$ hours. Serve sprinkled with chopped parsley and accompanied by toasted cheese fingers.

5 LOW-COST MEAT DISHES

Some of the most enjoyable meals you have eaten abroad have quite possibly been based on cheap cuts of meat. It is the additional ingredients, and long unhurried cooking in many cases, which makes the difference.

Brisket, still comparatively cheap, is one of the tastiest joints you can buy, whether you want to eat it hot or cold. It may appear a little fatter than the topside or rump you would like to buy, but this helps to provide the delicious flavour. It needs no additional seasoning beyond salt, but it does need long slow cooking. Over-cooking doesn't matter, except to the carver if it is to be eaten hot. Let it cool if you wish and when you want to serve it just heat the gravy – adding only a little water to the juices (nothing else, to preserve that lovely flavour).

Other economical cuts are shin of beef, scrag end of mutton, breast of lamb, blade bone, spare rib and hand of pork. (Hand of pork not only makes a good joint for roasting but is a good buy if you want pork for a casserole or a pie; even allowing for the bone, it is more economical than most other cuts would be.) Then there are bacon joints, especially collar, forehock and knuckle, which make delicious main meals. Boiled forehock, on the bone, will still provide stock for soup after it has been served for a hot *and* a cold meal. Offal such as liver, kidneys and tripe can be enjoyed in many ways, too.

Casseroled beef balls
(*see picture overleaf*)

4 tbsps cooking oil (*60 ml*)
1 large onion, skinned and sliced
1 clove garlic, skinned and crushed
1 lb minced beef (*450 g*)
2 oz fresh white breadcrumbs (*50 g*)
2 tsps Worcestershire sauce (*10 ml*)
salt and pepper
1 egg, beaten
1 oz flour (*25 g*)

1 lb carrots, peeled and sliced (*450 g*)
1 lb potatoes, peeled (*450 g*)
14-oz can tomatoes (*400 g, approx*)
½ level tsp dried sage (*2.5 ml*)
1 bayleaf
1 pint beef stock (made with a cube) (*500 ml*)
parsley for garnish

(Serves 4)

Heat 2 tbsps (30 ml) oil in a frying pan, add the onion and fry until light golden brown. Add the garlic, drain and place in a 4½-pint (3-litre) casserole. Meanwhile, mix together the beef, crumbs, sauce, salt, pepper and egg. Work together, then form into 16 balls. Toss the beef balls in flour. Heat the remaining oil in the frying pan and fry meat balls until light golden brown (about 10 minutes). Add to the casserole with carrots.

Cut the potatoes into 1-in. (2½-cm) cubes. Add to the casserole with the tomatoes, sage, bayleaf and stock. Adjust seasoning, cover, and cook in centre of oven at 350 °F (180 °C), mark 4, for 1½ hours. Serve sprinkled with chopped parsley.

Casseroled beef balls

Navarin of lamb (*page 54*)

Thrifty beef pie
(*see photograph on front cover*)

1¼ lb shin of beef (*550 g*)
1 oz plain flour (*25 g*)
salt and pepper
2 oz dripping or lard (*50 g*)
8 oz onions, skinned and
　chopped (*225 g*)
8 oz carrots, peeled and cut into
　chunks (*225 g*)
6 oz parsnips, peeled and cut into
　chunks (*175 g*)

3 oz dried butter beans, soaked
　overnight (*75 g*)
¾ pint beef stock (*400 ml*)
2 level tsps tomato paste (*10 ml*)
2 tsps Worcestershire
　sauce (*10 ml*)
1 level tsp dried mixed herbs (*5 ml*)
7-oz packet frozen puff pastry,
　thawed (*200 g*)
1 egg, beaten

(Serves 4–5)

Trim the meat and cut it into 1-in. (2½-cm) pieces. Toss in seasoned flour.
Heat 1 oz (25 g) dripping or lard in a large pan and briskly fry half the meat
until brown on all sides. Drain and place in a casserole. Fry the rest of the meat,

53

drain and add to the casserole. Heat the remaining dripping or lard and quickly fry the onions, carrots and parsnips, until beginning to brown. Stir in any remaining flour and gradually add the stock, tomato paste, Worcestershire sauce, herbs and seasoning. Bring to the boil and pour over the meat in the casserole. Drain the butter beans and add to the casserole. Stir all the ingredients together. Cook in the oven at 325 °F (170 °C), mark 3, for 2–2½ hours, until tender. Cool quickly.

Turn the meat into a 2-pint (1-litre) pie dish. Roll out the pastry and use it to cover the pie, using any trimmings to make decorations. At this stage the pie may be left if you wish, in a cool place, until required.

To bake the pie, brush with beaten egg and bake at 425 °F (220 °C), mark 7, for about 20 minutes until golden. Reduce the heat to 350 °F (180 °C), mark 4, and cook for a further 20 minutes. Cover the pastry lightly with foil if it starts to overbrown.

Beef roulades

1½ lb lean minced beef (*600 g*)
1 large egg
salt and pepper
¼ level tsp oregano (*2.5 ml*)
6 oz mature Cheddar cheese, grated (*150 g*)

½ oz lard or dripping (*15 g*)
14-oz can whole tomatoes (*396 g*)
2 oz onion, skinned and grated (*50 g*)
¼ pint water (*150 ml*)
chopped parsley

(Serves 4–6)

Work the meat with the egg, salt, pepper and oregano. Divide into 4. On a floured board, pat each portion out to a 6-in. (15-cm) square. Cover each with a quarter of the cheese. Roll up firmly and cut in half crosswise. Fry the meat briskly but carefully, until golden-brown, in the melted fat. Transfer to a casserole. Add the canned tomatoes and their juice to the pan with the onion and water. Bring to the boil, season and pour over the meat. Cover with a lid and cook in the oven at 325 °F (170 °C), mark 3, for about an hour. To serve, sprinkle with parsley.

Navarin of lamb

(*see picture page 53*)

2–2½ lb best end of neck or shoulder of lamb (*900 g*)
½ oz fat or 2 tbsps cooking oil (*10–15 g fat or 30 ml oil*)
1 level tsp sugar (*5 ml*)
1 level tbsp flour (*15 ml*)
1½ pints stock or water (*375 ml*)
2 level tbsps tomato paste (*30 ml*)

salt and pepper
bouquet garni
4 onions, skinned and quartered
4 carrots, peeled and sliced
1–2 turnips, skinned and quartered
8 small, even sized potatoes, peeled

(Serves 4)

54

Trim the meat and cut into serving portions. Fry lightly on all sides in the fat or oil. Stir in the sugar and heat until it browns lightly, then add the flour, stirring until this cooks and browns. Remove from the heat, stir in the stock gradually, then bring to the boil and add the tomato paste, seasonings and bouquet garni. Add the onions, carrots and turnips and continue cooking for another 30 minutes. Finally add the potatoes and continue cooking for 20 minutes, until tender.

Roast stuffed breast of lamb
(*see picture overleaf*)

1 lb breast of lamb (*450 g*)
salt
freshly ground black pepper
lemon juice
flour to coat joint
½ oz dripping (*15 g*)

For the stuffing
½ oz dripping (*15 g*)
½ an onion
½ lb sausage meat (*200 g*)
2 tsps chopped parsley (*10 ml*)
3 tbsps fresh white
  breadcrumbs (*45 ml*)

(Serves 2–3)

Wipe the breast of lamb and sprinkle the inside with salt, pepper and lemon juice. Spread the stuffing (see below) over the meat. Roll up loosely and tie in several places with string. Weigh the joint. Season the flour and rub into the surface of the lamb. Melt the dripping in a roasting tin and put in the meat.

Roast in the centre of the oven at 350 °F (180 °C), mark 4, for 27–30 minutes per lb plus 27 minutes (30–35 minutes per 450 g, plus 35 minutes). Baste once or twice. Either serve hot, with gravy, or allow to become quite cold, then slice and serve with salad.

For the stuffing: Melt the dripping in a pan, add the chopped onion and fry gently until soft but not coloured. Add the sausage meat, parsley and breadcrumbs and mix well.

Lancashire hot pot
(*see picture page 57*)

8 middle neck lamb chops
½ lb onions, skinned and sliced (*200 g*)
2 lamb's kidneys, skinned and diced
  (optional)

1 lb potatoes, peeled and cut into
  chunks (*450 g*)
salt and pepper
½ pint stock (*250 ml*)
1 oz lard or dripping (*25 g*)

(Serves 4)

Remove any excess fat from the chops and place them in a casserole. Add the onions, the kidneys if used, and lastly the potato; season well. Pour on the stock and brush the top of the potato with melted lard or dripping. Cover and cook in the centre of the oven at 325 °F (170 °C), mark 3, for 2 hours, or until the meat and potatoes are tender. For the last 20 minutes of cooking time remove the lid to allow the potatoes to brown.

Cawl mamgu

1 lb middle neck of lamb (*450 g*)
salt
freshly ground black pepper
½ lb small carrots, peeled and
    halved (*200 g*)
1 small swede, peeled and sliced

1 large leek, cleaned
½ lb potatoes, peeled and
    quartered (*200 g*)
½ oz flour (*15 ml*)
½ oz parsley, chopped (*15 ml*)

(Serves 4–6)

Roast stuffed breast of lamb (*page 55*)

Lancashire hot pot (*page 55*)

Put the chopped meat, still on the bone but trimmed of excess fat, into a saucepan. Cover with cold water. Season well with salt and pepper and bring slowly to the boil. Skim the surface carefully. Add the carrots, the swede and just the white part of the leek. Simmer gently, covered, for 1–1½ hours. Add the potatoes, and the green of the leek cut into fine shreds. Continue to simmer for a further 15–20 minutes. When the potatoes are almost cooked, thicken with flour and a little water blended together to a cream. Cook for a further 5 minutes. Add the parsley. Serve in bowls.

Frikadeller

For the dumplings
3 oz fresh white breadcrumbs (75 g)
⅜ pint milk (250 ml)
8 oz pie veal, minced (200 g)
8 oz pork, minced (200 g)
1 egg, beaten
salt and pepper

For the stock
1¾ pints water (1 litre)
2 level tsps salt (10 ml)
6 white peppercorns
1 bayleaf
parsley
1 onion, skinned
1 small carrot, peeled

(Serves 4)

Soak the breadcrumbs in the milk. Mix together the minced meats; stir in the beaten egg, salt and pepper. Add the soaked breadcrumbs and work the mixture until smooth. (It will be fairly soft.)

Put the stock ingredients into a saucepan and bring to the boil. Shape the meat mixture into small balls, using two teaspoons. Add the little dumplings a few at a time to the stock and let them simmer for 7–10 minutes. Serve hot, with tomato sauce, or with a lemon and tarragon sauce, and boiled rice.

Osso bucco
(see picture page 65)

2 lb shin of veal (4 pieces) (900 g)
salt and pepper
2 oz margarine (50 g)
1 medium onion, skinned and finely chopped
2 carrots, peeled and thinly sliced
2 stalks celery, trimmed and thinly sliced
1 clove garlic, skinned and crushed
1 level tbsp flour (25 g)
½ pint chicken stock (250 ml)
¾ lb tomatoes, skinned and quartered (300 g)
pinch of dried rosemary
2 tbsps chopped parsley (30 ml)
grated rind 1 lemon

Season the veal with salt and pepper. Melt the margarine in a saucepan large enough to take the veal in one layer. Brown the veal, then put aside. If necessary, add a little more margarine before gently frying the onion, carrots and celery until they are just beginning to brown. Add the crushed garlic. Return the meat to the pan, add the flour and cook for a few minutes, then add the stock. Cover and cook gently for 1 hour. Transfer to a large shallow casserole. Add the tomatoes and rosemary, cover and continue to cook gently in the oven at 350 °F (180 °C), mark 4, for an hour, until the meat is tender. Sprinkle with parsley and lemon rind before serving.

If convenient, prepare the day before to the point where the meat is transferred to a casserole. Cool quickly and refrigerate.

Mince and bacon pie

$\frac{1}{4}$ lb streaky bacon rashers, rinded (100 g)
1 lb minced beef (400 g)
1 beef stock cube
1 level tbsp dried onion flakes (15 ml)
1 level tbsp dried celery flakes (15 ml)
2 level tbsps flour (30 ml)

$\frac{1}{2}$ pint water (250 ml)
gravy browning
salt and pepper
8 oz shortcrust pastry (8 oz flour, etc.) (200 g)
milk for glazing

(Serves 4 6)

Finely scissor-snip the bacon rashers into a frying pan. Cook slowly until the fat begins to run. Add the mince and continue to cook slowly until the beef is well separated and lightly browned. Crumble in the stock cube with the onion, celery and flour; stir and slowly add the water. Bring to the boil, reduce heat and simmer for 20 minutes. Add browning to give a rich brown. Adjust the seasoning and cool.

Roll out about half the pastry to line an 8-in. (20-cm) metal pie plate. Add the cooled filling and cover with the remaining pastry rolled out to fit. Brush with milk. Bake in the oven at 400 °F (200 °C), mark 6, for about 45 minutes. Serve with a green vegetable.

Bacon in cider

2 lb collar joint (1 kg)
1 bayleaf
1 large onion, skinned and chopped

$\frac{1}{2}$ pint dry cider (300 ml)
1 level tsp cornflour (5 ml)

(Serves 6)

String the bacon joint and soak it for about 4 hours. Drain, place in a saucepan and cover with fresh cold water. Bring to the boil, pour off the water and cover again with fresh water. Add the bayleaf; bring to the boil, cover, reduce heat and simmer for half the cooking time (20 minutes per lb (450 g) plus 20 minutes).

Remove the joint from the cooking liquid. Peel away the rind and place the meat in a casserole with the chopped onion and cider. Cook, covered, at 375 °F (190 °C), mark 5, for the rest of the cooking time. Baste 2 or 3 times with

Chipstead churdles *(page 66)*, pan haggerty *(page 78)* and faggots *(page 64)*

cider liquor. To serve, slice the bacon and keep it warm while thickening the juices with cornflour. Cook 1–2 minutes and pour over the bacon.

Blanquette of rabbit

2 lb rabbit joints (1 kg)
6 oz lean bacon, rinded and diced (150 g)
1 large onion, skinned
1 clove
1 clove garlic, skinned and crushed
bouquet garni
salt and black pepper
¼ pint white stock (150 ml)
1 tbsp lemon juice (15 ml)
cold water

1 oz margarine (25 g)
2 level tbsps flour (30 ml)
2 egg yolks
3 tbsps cream or top of the milk (50 ml)

For garnish
8 small onions, sautéed
8 button mushrooms, sautéed
chopped parsley
4 small slices white bread, fried

(Serves 4–6)

Chop each joint in two. Put with the bacon, clove-studded onion, garlic bouquet garni and seasoning in a large pan. Add the stock, lemon juice and enough water just to cover. Bring to the boil, skim, cover and simmer until the rabbit is really tender and leaving the bone – about 1½ hours. Strain of the liquid, discard the onion and bouquet garni. Keep the rabbit warm in a clean casserole. Melt the fat, stir in the flour and cook for 2 minutes. Gradually add 1 pint (500 ml) of the cooking liquor, bring to the boil and simmer for 2–3 minutes, stirring. Beat the egg yolks and cream together and slowly add the warm – not hot – stock. Adjust seasoning and re-heat, but do not boil Pour the sauce over the rabbit and add the sautéed onions and mushrooms Garnish with parsley and arrange triangles of fried bread around the edge.

Rabbit casserole

4 rabbit joints
1 oz seasoned flour (25 g)
1 lb potatoes, peeled (450 g)

2–3 onions, skinned and sliced
chopped parsley
stock or water

(Serves 4)

Wash the rabbit joints, dry and toss in the flour. Cut the potatoes into chips 2 in. (5 cm) long. Place a layer of onion in a casserole. Put the rabbit on top, sprinkle liberally with parsley and cover with onion and potato. Add the liquid, nearly covering the rabbit; put the lid on and bake for 2–2½ hours at 325 °F (170 °C), mark 3. Remove the lid a short time before serving, to brown the potatoes.

Braised sweetbreads

lb lambs' sweetbreads, fresh or
  frozen (450 g)
large carrot, peeled and diced
onion, skinned and diced
stalks celery, trimmed and sliced
tbsp corn oil (15 ml)

salt and pepper
½ pint white stock (300 ml)
2–3 oz green streaky bacon rashers,
  rinded (50–75 g)
3 level tsps cornflour (15 ml)
parsley to garnish

(Serves 4)

Soak the sweetbreads for at least 4 hours, changing the water several times.
Put into fresh cold water and bring slowly to the boil. Lift out the sweetbreads,
using a draining spoon, and rinse under running cold water. Remove the black
veins and skin. Wrap lightly in a cloth or muslin and cool, pressed between
two weighted plates.

Sauté the prepared vegetables in oil until half cooked. Place them in the
base of a casserole just large enough to take the sweetbreads. Add seasoned
stock just to cover and arrange the sliced sweetbreads on top. Overlap the
bacon rashers on the sweetbreads. Cover and cook at 375 °F (190 °C), mark 5,
for 30–45 minutes, basting occasionally. Increase the temperature to 425 °F
(220 °C), mark 7, and remove the lid for the last 10 minutes.

Strain the liquor from the casserole and thicken with cornflour. Pour over
the sweetbreads and garnish with parsley.

Lancashire tripe and onions

lb dressed tripe (450 g)
lb shallots or small onions (200 g)
pint milk (500 ml)
oz butter or margarine (25 g)

½ oz flour (15 ml)
pinch salt
freshly ground black pepper
pinch ground nutmeg

(Serves 4)

Wash the tripe and cut it into strips. Boil some water, pour it over the onions,
allow to stand for a few minutes and drain before peeling the onions. Put the
tripe, onions and milk in a saucepan; simmer gently, uncovered, for 1–1½
hours or until tender. Melt the butter, stir in the flour and cook the roux for
1–2 minutes. Remove from the heat. Strain the milk from the tripe after
cooking, gradually add it to the roux, blending them together until smooth.
Season well with salt, pepper and nutmeg. Let the sauce simmer for about 5
minutes, stirring. Add the tripe and onions to the sauce and re-heat before
placing in a serving dish. Serve with creamed potatoes.

Somerset tripe

2 lb dressed tripe (*1 kg*)
1 large onion, skinned and chopped
3 tbsps cooking oil (*45 ml*)
1 bayleaf
¼ pint dry cider (*150 ml*)
6½-oz can tomatoes (*about 185 g*)

1 clove garlic, skinned
pinch each of rosemary and nutmeg
1 tbsp chopped parsley (*15 ml*)
2 level tsps beef extract (*10 ml*)
¼ pint water (*100 ml*)
salt and freshly ground black pepper

(Serves 6)

Cut the tripe into fine strips. Fry the onion until golden in the oil, then add the bayleaf and cider. Cover the pan and cook slowly until the cider is well reduced. Add the tripe, tomatoes with their juice, crushed garlic, rosemary, nutmeg, parsley, and beef extract dissolved in the water. Season, cover and cook gently for 1 hour. Remove the tripe from its juices, using a draining spoon. Reduce the juices by fast boiling to ½ pint (250 ml), then return the tripe and reheat. Serve with more chopped parsley.

Liver casserole

1 lb liver (*450 g*)
2 level tbsps seasoned flour (*30 ml*)
6 rashers of bacon, rinded and chopped

4 onions, skinned and sliced
2 oz fat or oil (*50 g*)
14-oz can tomatoes (*400 g approx.*)
1 tbsp Worcestershire sauce (*15 ml*)

(Serves 4)

Wash the liver and remove any skin or tubes; cut into even-sized pieces and coat with the seasoned flour. Fry it with the bacon and onions in the hot fat or oil until just brown. Place in a casserole with the tomatoes and sauce, cover and cook in the centre of the oven at 350 °F (180 °C), mark 4, for 45 minutes, or until the liver is tender.

Faggots

(*see picture page 61*)

1 lb pig's liver (*400 g*)
6 oz onion, skinned (*150 g*)
10 oz fresh white breadcrumbs (*250 g*)
3 oz shredded suet (*75 g*)
salt

freshly ground black pepper
½ level tsp chopped sage (*2.5 ml*)
1 level tbsp flour (*15 ml*)
1 pint dark rich beef stock (*500 ml*)
chopped parsley

(Serves 4–6)

Mince the liver and onion together, add the breadcrumbs and suet and combine fully together. Season well with salt, pepper and sage. Shape into balls

Osso bucco (*page 58*)

on a well floured surface. Place each faggot in a small square of buttered foil. Enclose them loosely and place on a baking sheet. Bake in centre of oven at 350 °F (180 °C), mark 4, for about 30 minutes. Remove the faggots from the foil; place them in a flameproof casserole. To make the gravy, place the flour in a small bowl and blend to a cream with a little of the stock. Add remaining stock and pour round the faggots. Heat gently, turning the faggots, until the gravy thickens. Cook for 5–10 minutes, then garnish with parsley and serve. *Note:* Foil replaces the caul which was originally used but is now difficult to obtain.

Chipstead churdles

(see picture page 60)

For filling
1 oz dripping (25 g)
1 onion, skinned and chopped
6 oz lamb's liver (150 g)
6 oz bacon, rinded (150 g)
2 oz mushrooms, chopped (50 g)
1 small cooking apple, peeled and
  chopped
1 tbsp chopped parsley (15 ml)

salt
freshly ground black pepper

8 oz shortcrust pastry (8 oz flour,
  etc.) (200 g)
1 level tbsp browned breadcrumbs
  (15 ml)
1 level tbsp grated cheese (15 ml)

(Makes 6)

Melt the dripping in a pan, lightly fry the onion and liver, then mince finely with the bacon. Add the chopped mushrooms and apple, parsley and seasonings. Roll out the pastry, invert a saucer as a guide and cut 6 pastry circles, about 5½-in. (14-cm) diameter. Brush the outside edge with water or milk. Divide the filling mixture between the six circles. Turn up the edges to make tricorn shapes, leaving the centres exposed. Pinch together and flute the edges and brush the pastry with milk. Combine the crumbs and cheese, sprinkle over churdles and bake at 375 °F (190 °C), mark 5, for about 40 minutes. Serve hot.

6 HOME-MADE DELICATESSEN

Don't just drool over the displays at the delicatessen counter; go home and make something for yourself. Home-made pâtés and terrines are by no means as expensive as the ones which grace the display counter of the more exclusive food halls, but are just as enjoyable. If you have a freezer you can make extra, even more economical, quantities and store them in conveniently sized servings.

Parslied ham
(*see picture page 72*)

2 lb gammon, lean collar or
    forehock (*1 kg*)
knuckle of veal, chopped
1 calf's foot, chopped
1 level tsp dried chervil (*5 ml*)
1 level tsp dried tarragon (*5 ml*)
bayleaf
few sprigs of parsley
(Serves 6–8)

6 peppercorns
1 pint dry white wine or dry
    cider (*500 ml*)
½ pint water (*250 ml*)
salt and pepper
2 tsps lemon juice (*10 ml*)
3 tbsps chopped parsley (*45 ml*)

In a saucepan, cover the gammon with water. Bring to the boil, reduce heat and simmer for 45 minutes. Drain the gammon, discard the rind and cut the meat into pieces. Return to the pan, adding the veal and calf's foot. Tie the chervil, tarragon, bayleaf, parsley and peppercorns in muslin and place them in the pan with the wine (or cider) and water. Cover tightly and bring to the boil; skim if necessary. Reduce heat and simmer until really tender. Discard the muslin bag and strain the liquor through more muslin. Adjust seasoning and add the lemon juice. Flake the gammon with a fork and place it in a stone jar or 1½-pint (700-ml) pudding basin. Add the chopped parsley to the cooking liquor and pour it over the ham. Leave in a cold place to jell and unmould.

Pressed tongue

(see picture page 72)

1 salted ox tongue, approx 3 lb (*1.5 kg*)
8 peppercorns
1 carrot, peeled and sliced

1 onion, skinned and studded with
   3 cloves
1 bayleaf

(Serves 10–12)

Wash the tongue; allow to soak for 24 hours if highly salted. Put it into a saucepan, just cover with cold water and top with a lid. Bring to the boil, remove any scum with a spoon and add peppercorns, carrots, onion and bayleaf. Cover the pan and bring to the boil again, reduce heat and simmer the tongue until tender – about 3 hours. As a rough guide, allow 1 hour per lb (450 g). Plunge tongue briefly into cold water when it is cooked.

    Ease off the skin while the tongue is still hot and remove the small bones from the back of the tongue. Return meat to the cooking liquor to cool. Curl the tongue into a round soufflé dish or deep cake tin lined with foil. The container should be such a size as to take the tongue leaving few gaps. Just cover the meat with cool strained cooking liquor and press either with a plate, heavily weighted, or with a tongue press. Chill until the juices have jellied.

Raised pie

(see picture page 72)

¾ lb lamb's liver (*350 g*)
¾ lb lean pork (*350 g*)
1 lb pork sausagemeat (*400 g*)
finely grated rind of 1 orange
2 tbsps chopped parsley (*30 ml*)
pinch ground cloves
½ level tsp dried sage (*2.5 ml*)
2 level tsps salt (*10 ml*)
freshly ground black pepper

For the pastry
1 lb plain flour (*500 g*)
2 level tsps salt (*10 ml*)
4 oz lard (*120 g*)
⅓ pint water (*180 ml*)
beaten egg, to glaze

(Serves 8)

Mince the liver and pork and work them into the sausagemeat with the orange rind, parsley, cloves, sage, salt and pepper. Sift the flour and salt into a bowl. Melt the lard slowly in water in a pan. Boil it and pour on to the flour. Work to a dough and knead. Grease a long loaf tin (13 in. by 4½ in. by 2½ in. – 33 cm by 11.5 cm by 6.5 cm – 3½-pint, 2-litre capacity) and line with two-thirds of the pastry. Spoon the meat into the centre and brush the pastry rim with beaten egg. Roll out remaining pastry to make a lid. Seal the edges and use the trimmings for decoration.

Make a hole in the centre. Brush the pastry with beaten egg and bake at 400 °F (200 °C), mark 6, for 20 minutes, then at 350 °F (180 °C), mark 4, for about 1 hour 40 minutes. Remove the pie from the oven, allow to cool and, when cold, fill the hole with well seasoned jellied stock or aspic jelly. Leave until set.

Cherry-stuffed veal

(see picture page 72)

7 lb breast of veal, boned (about
  5 lb after boning) (3.5 kg, 2.5 kg)
½ lb lean back bacon, in a piece (200 g)
5 oz glacé cherries (150 g)

sprigs of rosemary
cooking oil
garlic, salt, or 1 clove garlic and
  ordinary salt

Serves 12)

Lay the veal on a chopping board. Cut into the meat where it tapers; pull back flap to make an oblong shape. Remove the rind from the bacon, cut the bacon in quarters along the length of the rinded fat, and then in half at right angles to the first cut. Lay the strips of bacon at intervals along the veal, parallel to the long side. Position the cherries between the bacon with the rosemary. Roll up from the short side. Secure the roll with skewers before tying neatly and firmly with string.

Place the veal in a small roasting tin, brush over with oil and dust with garlic salt or halve a peeled clove of garlic and rub over the skin, then dust with salt. Roast at 400 °F (200 °C), mark 6, for 30 minutes; reduce temperature to 350 °F (180 °C), mark 4, and cook for about a further 2½ hours. Cover with foil or 2 layers of greaseproof paper, previously wetted, if meat is in danger of over-browning.

Brawn

(see picture page 72)

1 pig's head, salted and halved
2 pig's trotters
1½ lb shin of beef (600 g)
1 large bouquet garni
1 large onion, skinned

1 level tsp *quatre épices* (mixture of
  ground pepper, nutmeg, cloves,
  cinnamon or ginger to taste) (5 ml)
thinly pared rind of 1 lemon
browned breadcrumbs (optional)

(Serves 6–8)

Rinse the pig's head and trotters in cold water and put into a large pan with the beef, bouquet garni, onion, quatre épices and lemon rind. Barely cover with water. Cover with a tightly fitting lid, bring to the boil, reduce heat and simmer for $2\frac{1}{2}$–3 hours or until head and skin are very tender. Cool a little, then lift the meat on to a large dish.

Remove the flesh from the head, discarding any excess fat. Return the bones to the liquor and reduce, by boiling, to about 1 pint (500 ml). Skim off fat. Dice all the meat finely and place in a $3\frac{1}{2}$-pint (2-litre) pudding basin. Adjust seasoning of the stock and strain it over the meat just to cover. Leave overnight in a cold place. To serve, leave plain or coat with browned breadcrumbs.

Rillettes de porc

(see picture page 72)

2 lb belly or neck of pork, rinded and
   boned (*1 kg*)
salt
1 lb back pork fat (*450 g*)

1 clove garlic, skinned and bruised
bouquet garni
freshly ground black pepper

(Serves 4–6)

Rub the meat well with salt and leave it to stand for 4–6 hours. Then cut it into thin strips along the grooves from where the bones were removed. Put these strips into an earthenware or other oven dish, with the pork fat also cut into small strips. Bury a bruised clove of garlic and a bouquet garni in the centre, season with a little pepper; add 3 fl. oz (75 ml) water. Cover with a lid and cook at 300 °F (150 °C), mark 2, for about 4 hours. Discard the bouquet garni and garlic, season well. Strain the fat from the meat and when well drained, partly pound it then pull into fine shreds with two forks. Pile lightly into a glazed earthenware or china jar. Pour the fat over the top. Cover with foil. Keep in a cool place.

Rillettes should be soft-textured, so allow to come to room temperature before serving.

Spicy meat loaf

$\frac{1}{2}$ lb beef, minced (*200 g*)
$\frac{1}{4}$ lb sausagemeat (*100 g*)
$\frac{1}{4}$ lb lean bacon, rinded and
   minced (*100 g*)
2 oz fresh white breadcrumbs (*50 g*)
6 oz onion, skinned and chopped (*150 g*)

$\frac{1}{4}$ level tsp mixed spice (*1.25 ml*)
1 level tsp dried thyme (*5 ml*)
salt and pepper
1 egg, beaten
3 bayleaves

(Serves 4–6)

Mix together beef, sausagemeat and bacon. Add the breadcrumbs, onion, mixed spice, thyme, salt and pepper. Mix thoroughly, and bind with the egg. Grease a $1\frac{1}{4}$-pint (700-ml) loaf tin. Place bayleaves in the bottom and spoon in the meat mixture and press well down. Cover with greased foil. Place on a baking sheet and bake at 325 °F (170 °C), mark 3, for 2 hours. Turn out of tin and serve hot or cold.

Simple chicken liver pâté

2 oz butter (*50 g*)
2 bayleaves
pinch of dried thyme
1 small onion, skinned and chopped

1 lb chicken livers (*400 g*)
salt and pepper
melted butter to cover

(Serves 4–6)

Melt the butter in a pan. Add the bayleaves, thyme and onion and cook gently for 2–3 minutes. Prepare the chicken livers and cut each into 2–3 pieces. Add to the pan and simmer gently for 5–7 minutes until livers are cooked. Remove bayleaves. Mince the livers once or twice, using a fine grinder (the second mincing gives a smoother pâté). Season well and divide between 4–6 individual dishes, or put in one large one. Pour a little melted butter over the top and chill until set.

Meat pâté
(*see picture page 72*)

1½ lb lamb's liver (*600 g*)
½ lb chicken livers (*200 g*)
½ lb lean veal (*200 g*)
1 lb belly pork, rinded and boned (*400 g*)
4 oz onions, skinned (*100 g*)
2 cloves garlic, skinned

2 level tsps salt (*10 ml*)
½ level tsp freshly ground black pepper (*2.5 ml*)
1 level tsp basil (*5 ml*)
2 tbsps brandy or lemon juice (*30 ml*)
½ lb streaky bacon rashers, rinded (*200 g*)

(Serves 8–10)

Mince lamb and chicken livers, veal, pork, onion and garlic once. Blend in the salt, pepper, basil and brandy or lemon juice. Stretch the bacon rashers by drawing the blade of a knife along the length of the rashers and use these to line the base and sides of a 3½–4-pint (1.5–2-litre) capacity loaf tin or similar sized ovenproof dish or terrine. Spoon in the minced meats; cover with more bacon. Place the pâté in a roasting tin with 1 in. (3 cm) depth of water. Lightly top with foil and cook in the oven at 350 °F (180 °C), mark 4, for 2½–3 hours. When cool, weight down and leave until cold in the refrigerator or another cool place.

Home-made delicatessen

Thrifty pâté

1¼ lb lean belly pork (*500 g*)
½ lb pig's or ox liver (*200 g*)
¼ lb lean streaky bacon, rinded (*100 g*)
4 oz onion, skinned and chopped (*100 g*)
1 small clove garlic, skinned and
  crushed

1 level tsp salt (*5 ml*)
freshly ground black pepper
1 oz butter (*25 g*)

(Serves 6)

Remove the rind and any bones from the pork and dice it. Rinse the liver under cold running water, dry on absorbent paper and cut into largish pieces. Mince the meats, onion and garlic together three times. Work in the salt and pepper. Turn into a 2-pint (1-litre) terrine or small casserole and lightly top with foil, or a lid. Place in a small roasting tin half full of water. Bake for about 1½ hours at 300 °F (150 °C), mark 2. Remove the lid, lay a double sheet of foil over the top, add weights and weight down until quite cold, preferably in a refrigerator. Remove weights and covering, melt the butter over a low heat, pour over pâté and chill. Serve with warm-from-the-oven granary bread.

Kipper pâté
(*see picture opposite*)

12 oz kipper fillets (frozen) (*300 g*)
½–1 clove garlic
8 oz butter and margarine (half and
  half) (*200 g*)

juice of 1 lemon
yolk of 1 hardboiled egg

(Fills 6–8 small ramekin dishes)

Put the bag of frozen kipper fillets in boiling water for 1 minute. Remove the fillets and remove any skin. Skin and chop the garlic; pound the fish with the garlic, butter and margarine, lemon juice and egg yolk. Turn the mixture into a soufflé dish or 6–8 ramekin dishes and chill. Serve with toast triangles and sprigs of watercress.

Brandade of kipper

1 lb kipper fillets (*400 g*)
1 small clove garlic, skinned and
  crushed
6 tbsps olive oil (*90 ml*)

3 tbsps single cream or top of the
  milk (*45 ml*)
salt and freshly ground black pepper

Poach the fillets, then drain and skin them. Put in a saucepan and beat with a wooden spoon to break up the flesh. Beat in the crushed clove of garlic and heat

Kipper pâté (*opposite*)

gently, stirring. Stir in the olive oil gradually, beating between each addition. Follow with the cream. Remove from the heat and adjust seasoning. Press lightly into small pots and chill. Serve with lemon wedges.

Rollmops

(*see picture page 72*)

(*see picture page 72*)

8 herrings, cleaned
3 oz salt (*75 g*)
1 pint water (*500 ml*)
2 oz onion, skinned and finely
   sliced (*50 g*)

For the pickle
2 pints cider vinegar (*1 litre*)
4 whole allspice, crushed
2 bayleaves
3 oz sugar, optional (*75 g*)

(Serves 8)

Run the thumb along the backbone to ease the bones away from the flesh, spread out the fish and lift away the whole backbone, prising with the thumb of

75

one hand and the fingers of the other. Use a pointed knife to remove the small bones. Leave the herrings in the salt and water for 3 hours. Drain well, roll up towards the tail and secure with cocktail-sticks. Leave the herrings overnight in the pickle with the onion.

To make the pickle: Bring to the boil the vinegar, allspice, bayleaf and sugar. Allow to get cold. Strain.

Potted cheese

4 oz butter or margarine (*100 g*)
pinch ground mace
¼ level tsp dry mustard (*1.25 ml*)

2–3 tbsps dry sherry (*30–45 ml*)
10 oz Cheshire cheese, grated (*250 g*)

Cream the butter or margarine, mace, mustard and sherry until really soft. Slowly beat in the cheese. Serve in small earthenware pots. (This will keep for a fortnight in the refrigerator.)

7 MAINLY MEATLESS

here is no reason why every meal should have a meat-and-two-veg main
urse. Don't forget the great potential of vegetables as main course
gredients. One of the easiest ways to present a vegetable – such as celery,
bbage, cauliflower and leeks – in this way is to top it with a cheese sauce,
en with a little grated cheese and crumbs, and flash it under the grill. But
ere are times when something more substantial, more interesting, is needed –
d not necessarily a wholly vegetable casserole or the 'Woolton pie' which
d so many families during the last war. This chapter includes recipes intro-
cing cheese and eggs as well as vegetables as main ingredients, and some
eas using a little meat – comparatively speaking – along with the other
gredients.

Root vegetables – parsnips, carrots, swedes and turnips – can make good
ain courses. Try beetroot cooked whole and served hot with crumbly bacon
d a cheese sauce. Crisp winter cabbage, shredded finely, makes a good base
r salads when lettuce prices itself beyond your budget. It is delicious, too, if
anched with a little chopped onion, seasoning and butter and then topped
ith a poached egg. Very ripe tomatoes can be a good buy if you are going to
ok them immediately, and misshapen ones are usually cheaper than
rfectly shaped ones. Don't dismiss end-of-season unripe tomatoes as useless;
ey're fine for green tomato pickles.

Eggs and cheese are always good value for money – even though they are
ore expensive than they used to be. Eggs still make comparatively low-cost
ain meal dishes, in soufflés, omelettes and quiches, and have almost un-
mited possibilities in quick snacks. Top Welsh rarebit, baked beans or
aghetti – all on toast – with a poached or fried egg for extra nourishment.

Pan hagerty

(see picture page 60)

1 lb potatoes (400 g)
8 oz onions (200 g)
1 oz dripping (25 g)

4 oz Cheddar cheese (100 g)
salt and freshly ground black pepper

(Serves 4)

Peel the potates and onions and cut them into thin slices. In an 8-in. (20-cm
shallow frying pan, melt the dripping and gently swirl around the edges
Layer the potatoes, onions and grated cheese alternately in the pan, seasoning
well between each layer. Finish with grated cheese on top and overlap potatoe
round the edge. Cover with a lid, then let the contents fry gently for about
30 minutes until the onions and potatoes are nearly cooked. Remove the lic
and brown the top under a hot grill. Serve straight from the pan.

Marrow and tomato medley

1 onion, skinned and chopped
1 oz butter or cooking oil (25 g)
1 medium sized marrow, peeled and
  diced

15-oz can tomatoes (about 425 g)
salt and pepper
mixed herbs

(Serves 2–4)

Fry the onion in butter for about 3–5 minutes until soft but not browned. Add
the marrow, tomatoes and their juice, seasoning and herbs and continue
cooking over a very low heat until the marrow is soft – about 45 minutes.

Casseroled stuffed marrow

1 medium sized marrow
4 oz onions, skinned and
  chopped (100 g)
1½ oz dripping (40 g)
2 level tbsps flour (30 ml)
12 oz lean cooked lamb or beef (300 g)

1 level tbsp tomato paste (15 ml)
1 level tsp Italian seasoning (5 ml)
2 tbsps chopped parsley (30 ml)
2 oz cooked long grain rice (50 g)
stock
salt and pepper

(Serves 4)

Peel the marrow, cut it in half lengthwise and scoop out the seeds. Blanch the
two halves in boiling water for 2–3 minutes and drain well. Brown the onion
in half the dripping until deep golden brown; stir in the flour and cook gently
for 2 minutes. Meanwhile, chop the meat finely (don't mince it). Add to the

nion with the tomato paste, seasoning, parsley, rice and enough stock to noisten. Bring to the boil, adjust seasoning and use to fill the marrow halves. ie the halves together, brush evenly all over with the remaining melted ripping. Place in a casserole, cover, and cook in oven at 350 °F (180 °C), mark , for 20 minutes. Baste and return to oven, uncovered, for a further 30 inutes. Drain off the juices and add to a good tomato sauce to serve hot as an ccompaniment.

Vegetable macaroni casserole

lb carrots, peeled (200 g)
small turnip, peeled
stalks celery, trimmed
leeks, trimmed and thoroughly
  cleaned
tomatoes, skinned
rasher bacon, rinded
oz dripping (25 g)

1 clove garlic, skinned and crushed
salt and pepper
$\frac{1}{4}$ pint tomato juice (150 ml)
2 oz macaroni (50 g)
4 tbsps chopped parsley (60 ml)
fried onion rings to garnish
grated cheese as accompaniment

Serves 2)

Cut up the vegetables and dice the bacon. Heat the fat and sauté first the bacon and then the vegetables for 10 minutes. Transfer to a casserole; add the garlic, seasoning and tomato juice and cook at 350 °F (180 °C), mark 4, for 1 hour. Meanwhile, cook the macaroni in boiling salted water until tender, drain and add with the parsley to the casserole and top with fried onion. Serve with cheese.

Mushroom casserole

onion, skinned and sliced into rings
oz butter or dripping (25 g)
sheep's kidney (optional)
lb mushrooms, wiped and
  sliced (300 g)

3 tomatoes, skinned and sliced
salt and pepper
1 tbsp chopped parsley (15 ml)
4 tbsps stock or water (60 ml)

Serves 2)

Grease a casserole. Fry the onion rings in fat until golden brown. Cut up the kidney, if used, and fill the dish with alternate layers of vegetables and kidney, seasoning well. Sprinkle with the parsley and finish with a layer of mushrooms. Add the liquid and stew gently in the oven at 350 °F (180 °C), mark 4, for about 30 minutes, or until tender. (Pack the ingredients closely to allow for shrinkage during cooking.)

Seasonal vegetables can make an excellent main course occasionally

Hot potato salad

4 rashers streaky bacon
1 small onion, skinned and diced
1 level tbsp flour *(15 ml)*
1 level tbsp sugar *(15 ml)*
1 level tsp salt *(5 ml)*
½ level tsp paprika *(2.5 ml)*

6 tbsps cider vinegar *(90 ml)*
7 tbsps water *(100 ml)*
2 eggs, hardboiled
4 cooked potatoes (1 ib) *(450 g)*
chopped parsley

(Serves 4)

80

Rind the bacon and snip it into ½-in. (1-cm) pieces. Fry slowly until the fat runs, then add the onion and cook until golden. Stir in the flour, sugar, salt, paprika, vinegar and water. Cook for about 2 minutes, stirring. Add the sliced eggs and cubed potatoes. Heat for about 10 minutes, stirring occasionally. Garnish with parsley when serving. This salad is good for supper with cold roast pork.

Cauliflower fondue

3 eggs
½ lb cauliflower florets (200 g)
2 tbsps milk (30 ml)
½ level tsp cornflour (2.5 ml)

few drops Worcestershire sauce
pinch salt and pepper
4 oz Cheddar cheese, grated (100 g)
1 tbsp chopped parsley (15 ml)

(Serves 2)

Hardboil one of the eggs. Cook the even-sized florets of cauliflower in salted water for about 10 minutes; they should be tender but still crisp. Drain. While the cauliflower is cooking, combine the milk, cornflour, Worcester sauce and seasoning in the top of a double boiler. (If care is taken, a small pan can be used over a low heat.) Heat until the cornflour thickens then add cheese. When the cheese melts, stir in the remaining two eggs, previously beaten, and continue to stir until the sauce thickens. Arrange the cauliflower in two individual, pre-heated earthenware dishes; spoon the sauce over. Garnish with chopped hardboiled egg mixed with parsley. Serve at once with toast fingers.

Stuffed jacket potatoes

6 large even-sized potatoes

For the curried egg filling
2 eggs, hardboiled
1 oz margarine (25 g)
2 oz onions, skinned and
    chopped (50 g)
2 oz cooking apple, peeled and
    diced (50 g)
½ level tsp curry powder (2.5 ml)
salt and pepper

For the bacon filling
1 oz margarine (25 g)
1 oz onion, skinned and chopped (25 g)
3 oz bacon rashers, rinded and
    chopped (75 g)
1 tbsp milk (15 ml)
½ level tsp dried marjoram (2.5 ml)
salt and pepper
4 oz Lancashire cheese, grated (100 g)

(Serves 6)

Wash, scrub and dry the potatoes. Prick with a fork, place on baking sheets and bake at 400 °F (200 °C), mark 6, for about 1 hour. Fill as described below and keep warm in a low oven.

For the curried egg filling: Sieve one of the hardboiled eggs. Melt the margarine in a pan and fry the onion until soft but not coloured. Add the apple and curry powder and fry for a further 5 minutes. Add the sieved egg. Cut a lid from 3 of the potatoes, scoop out the centre part and add to the curry mixture. Season well and replace inside the potato shells. Garnish with remaining hardboiled egg, sliced.

For the bacon filling: Melt the margarine, fry the onion until soft and put it aside. Add the bacon to the pan and fry until crisp. Scoop out the remaining 3 potatoes as above. Cream with the milk, add the onion, bacon and marjoram and season the mixture well. Re-fill the potato cases. Top with grated cheese and keep hot. Brown under a hot grill before serving.

Cheese and onion soufflé

3 eggs
1 oz butter or margarine (25 g)
2 oz onion, skinned and chopped (50 g)
1 oz plain flour (25 g)
¼ pint milk (150 ml)

3 oz mature Cheddar cheese,
  grated (75 g)
salt
freshly ground black pepper

(Serves 2–3)

Grease a 6-in. (15-cm) soufflé dish. Separate the eggs. Melt the butter, stir in onion and cook for 2–3 minutes until transparent. Add the flour and cook the roux for a few minutes. Gradually stir in the milk and bring to the boil, stirring all the time. Set aside to cool. Fold in the grated cheese. Add the egg yolks one at a time, beating well. Sprinkle over the seasoning. Stiffly whisk the egg whites, fold into the mixture and turn into the soufflé dish. Bake at 400 °F (200 °C), mark 6, for about 30–35 minutes until well risen and brown. Serve at once, with fingers of hot buttered toast.

Devilled sweetcorn

2 medium sized fresh corn cobs
4 oz butter or margarine, or half and
  half, softened (100 g)
4 level tbsps sweet pickle (60 ml)

1 tsp lemon juice (5 ml)
1 tsp chopped parsley (5 ml)
salt
freshly ground black pepper

(Serves 2)

Remove the beard and outer leaves from the cobs. Trim if necessary. Blanch for about 6 minutes, then drain. Combine the butter, pickle, lemon juice, parsley and seasoning together. Divide the mixture in half and spread on each

Butter bean quiche (page 84)

cob. Wrap them separately in kitchen foil and cook at 400 °F (200 °C), mark 6 for about 40 minutes until the corn is tender.

Note: Don't blanch the corn if prepared frozen cobs are used.

Butter bean quiche

(see picture page 83)

6 oz shortcrust pastry
  (6 oz flour etc.) *(150 g)*
1½ oz Cheddar cheese, grated *(40 g)*
2 eggs
½ pint milk *(250 ml)*

15-oz can butter beans, drained
  (420 g approx.)
salt and pepper
½ level tsp dried basil *(2.5 ml)*
2 tomatoes, skinned and sliced

(Serves 4)

Roll out the pastry and use it to line an 8½-in. (21-cm) flan ring. Sprinkle with three-quarters of the grated cheese. Beat the eggs lightly with the milk and add the butter beans. Season well with salt, pepper and basil. Pour the savoury custard over the cheese and arrange the slices of tomato on top. Sprinkle with the remaining cheese and bake at 400 °F (200 °C), mark 6, for 10 minutes. Reduce temperature to 350 °F (180 °C), mark 4, for a further 35 minutes. Serve with an apple and celery salad.

Cheese and corn double crust tart

8 oz shortcrust pastry
  (8 oz flour, etc.) *(200 g)*
4 oz streaky bacon rashers,
  rinded *(100 g)*

6 oz Lancashire cheese, grated *(150 g)*
11 oz creamed sweet corn *(about 312 g)*
pinch cayenne pepper
pinch freshly ground black pepper

(Serves 4–6)

Roll out the pastry and use half of it to line an 8-in. (20-cm) pie plate. Grill the bacon rashers and cut into snippets. Cover the pastry with half the cheese, then the corn mixed with the bacon, and then the remaining cheese. Season with cayenne and black pepper. Cover with a pastry lid. Bake at 325 °F (170 °C), mark 3, in the centre of the oven for about 1 hour. Serve hot.

Cheese creams

¼ pint aspic jelly (*150 ml*)
sliced radishes, cucumber or other garnish
½ oz powdered gelatine (*20 ml*)
3 oz cheese, grated (*75 g*)

salt
½ tsp made mustard (*2.5 ml*)
¼ pint white sauce (*125 ml*)
½ pint evaporated milk, chilled (*250 ml*)
cress for garnish

(Makes 6–8)

Put 1 tsp (5 ml) jelly in each dariole mould or small dish and allow to set. Garnish each with a radish or other colourful decoration, and cover this with a little more aspic. Dissolve the gelatine in any remaining aspic jelly and mix with the cheese, seasonings and sauce. Whip the milk until it is thick, and fold in. When the mixture is almost setting, pour into the moulds. Leave until set. Turn out to serve and garnish with cress.

8 INEXPENSIVE FISH DISHES

The deep freeze cabinet at the fishmonger's or supermarket may guarantee all-year-round availability of all kinds of fish at fairly constant prices, but there is still a lot to be said for buying it in season – providing you have a good supplier. Check prices first, of course; often there is little difference between fresh and frozen fish so far as cost is concerned; so you might conceivably prefer to pay a little more for the convenience of an out-of-season variety on occasions. If the fresh variety happens to cost a little more, though, it's often worth having nevertheless – just for the the flavour (providing it really is fresh) and serving with the minimum of trimmings.

The cheaper varieties of fresh fish are just as nourishing as the more expensive, and can be even tastier. Try serving rock salmon or whiting, for instance, in a well-flavoured batter; and if you can get sprats when they are in season, fry them or bake them with a savoury stuffing. Canned fish such as pilchards, herrings and tuna are useful, too, for lots of things other than sandwich fillings. Pilchards can generally be used where you would normally use the less economical sardines; or they can be added to a thick batter for delicious fritters. (Serve with freshly made tomato sauce.)

Tuna not only makes a very acceptable substitute for canned salmon in quiches and pies, but, mixed with a mushroom or parsley sauce, makes a delicious base for a potato-topped fisherman's pie.

North sea rice

1 lb cod fillet (*450 g*)
½ pint milk (*300 ml*)
bayleaf
salt and pepper
8 oz long grain rice (*200 g*)

2 eggs, hardboiled
rind and juice of 1 lemon
½ level tsp dried mixed herbs (*2.5 ml*)
1 tbsp chopped parsley (*15 ml*)
butter or margarine

(Serves 4)

Place the fish in a lidded frying pan with milk, bayleaf, salt and pepper.

Fish casserole (*page 90*)

Cover and simmer for 20 minutes. Drain the fish, remove the skin and any bones and flake the flesh. Meanwhile cook the rice in boiling salted water and drain. Roughly chop the hardboiled eggs. While fish and rice are really hot, toss together, add eggs, lemon rind and juice, mixed herbs and parsley. Serve at once in a hot casserole-type dish, dotted with butter or margarine.

Cod oriental

20 oz cod fillet, fresh or frozen (500 g)
1 tbsp lemon juice (15 ml)
flour
cooking oil
2 oz onion, skinned (50 g)
¼ lb tomatoes, skinned (100 g)

1 oz margarine (25 g)
1 level tbsp curry powder (15 ml)
1 level tbsp apple chutney (15 ml)
½ clove garlic
4 tbsps water (60 ml)
salt and pepper

(Serves 4)

Remove the skin from the cod and cut the fish into large pieces. Sprinkle lemon juice over, and leave for 15 minutes. Lightly dredge with flour. Just cover the base of a medium-sized frying pan with oil, heat and quickly fry the cod until brown. Keep on one side and wipe out the pan. Finely chop the onion and tomatoes. Melt the margarine and fry the onion gently with the curry powder for 5 minutes. Add chutney, garlic and water and simmer for about 5 minutes. Stir in the tomatoes, bring to the boil and add the fish. Turn carefully in the curry mixture, adjust seasoning and re-heat.

Thatched cod

1½ oz margarine (40 g)
4 fillets haddock or cod, 4–8 oz each
    (100–200 g each)
4 oz onions, skinned and
    chopped (100 g)
2 oz fresh white breadcrumbs (50 g)
2 oz mature Cheddar cheese, grated
    (50 g)

3 medium sized firm tomatoes,
    skinned and roughly chopped
salt
freshly ground black pepper
1 tbsp chopped parsley (15 ml)
rind and juice of 1 lemon
parsley sprigs

(Serves 4)

Melt half the fat in a small saucepan. Use a little to grease the inside of a shallow ovenproof serving dish. Arrange the fillets in a single layer and brush with the rest of the melted fat. Fry the onion in the remaining margarine without colouring. Combine with the breadcrumbs, cheese, tomatoes, salt, pepper, parsley, lemon rind and juice. Spoon evenly over the fillets and cook in the oven at 375 °F (190 °C), mark 5, for about 30 minutes. Garnish with parsley.

Russian fish pie

½ lb white fish (*225 g*)
1 oz margarine (*25 g*)
1 oz flour (*25 g*)
¼ pint milk (*125 ml*)
salt and pepper

2 tbsps chopped parsley (*30 ml*)
1 egg, hardboiled and chopped
4 oz bought flaky pastry (*100 g approx.*)
beaten egg to glaze

(Serves 4)

Wash the fish in cold water and remove the skin. Poach gently in salted water for 15 minutes then drain, retaining ¼ pint (125 ml) of the cooking liquid to make the sauce. Flake the fish when cooked. Melt the margarine, stir in the flour and cook for 2–3 minutes. Remove the pan from the heat and gradually stir in the fish liquid with the milk. Bring to the boil and continue to stir until the sauce thickens. Mix half the sauce with the flaked fish, salt, pepper, parsley and chopped egg. Roll out the pastry thinly into a fairly large square and place on a baking tray. Put the filling in the centre in a square, brush the edges of the pastry with beaten egg and draw them up to the middle, to form an envelope. Press the edges well together and flake and scallop them. Brush the pie with beaten egg and bake towards the top of the oven at 400 °F (200 °C), mark 6, for about 30 minutes, till golden. Serve with the remaining parsley sauce.

Fish pie Manitoba

1 lb cod or haddock fillet (*400 g*)
¼ lb streaky bacon rashers, rinded
   (*100 g*)
1 oz butter or margarine (*25 g*)
7-oz can corn kernels, drained
   (*about 198 g*)
½ pint milk (*250 ml*)

pared rind of 1 lemon
1 level tbsp cornflour (*15 ml*)
salt and pepper
1 tbsp chopped parsley (*15 ml*)
1½ lb old potatoes, boiled and
   creamed (*600 g*)

(Serves 4)

Skin the fish and cut the bacon into small pieces. Fry the bacon lightly until beginning to brown and the fat runs; add the butter and when melted add the fish and fry for a further 5–10 minutes. Flake the fish, add the corn, stir and turn into a 2-pint (1-litre) pie dish. Heat the milk, less 2 tbsps, with the lemon rind. Pour on to cornflour, blended with the reserved milk. Return to the pan and bring to the boil, stirring. Discard lemon rind, season the sauce well, add the parsley, and pour over the fish in the pie dish. In the meantime, prepare the potatoes and use to top the fish. Place the pie on a baking tray and cook towards the top of the oven at 425 °F (220 °C), mark 7, for about 30 minutes until golden brown and crisp.

Fish casserole

(see picture page 87)

1 lb white fish (*450 g*)
2 onions, skinned and chopped
½ pint tomato juice (*250 ml*)

salt and pepper
grated cheese

(Serves 4–5)

Skin and cut up the fish and place in a casserole. Sprinkle the chopped onion over the fish, cover with tomato juice and sprinkle with salt and pepper and then with grated cheese. Bake in the oven at 350 °F (180 °C), mark 4, for 45 minutes.

Goujons of whiting

1 lb boned and skinned whiting (*450 g*)
½ oz flour (*30 ml*)
1 large egg

salt and freshly ground black pepper
3 oz bought golden breadcrumbs (*75 g*)

(Serves 4)

With a sharp knife, cut the whiting into strips about 1 in. (2 cm) wide and 2 in. (5 cm) long. Sift the flour on to one plate, whisk the egg, salt and pepper on another and put the breadcrumbs on a final plate. Coat the fish in the flour, shake well; dip into the egg and allow excess to drip off. Finally coat in the breadcrumbs. Pat crumbs well in. Fry in deep fat a few pieces at a time at 360 °F (182 °C), for about 5 minutes. Drain well on absorbent paper; sprinkle with salt. Arrange on a serving plate and serve with lemon twists.

Soused mackerel

(see picture opposite)

5 even-sized mackerel
2 oz onion, skinned and sliced (*50 g*)
sprigs of parsley
2 bayleaves
pinch dried thyme
12 whole black peppercorns

½ level tsp salt (*2.5 ml*)
6 fl oz white wine vinegar (*150 ml*)
6 fl oz water (*150 ml*)
2 tbsps lemon juice (*30 ml*)
lemon slices and parsley for garnish

(Serves 5)

Remove the heads and gut the fish. Wash under cold running water and pat dry with absorbent kitchen paper. Lay the fish head to tail and side by side, in a shallow flameproof dish just big enough to hold them. Divide the onion slices into rings and arrange between and over the fish. Add the parsley sprigs,

Soused mackerel

bayleaves, thyme, peppercorns and salt. In a saucepan, bring the vinegar, water and lemon juice to the boil. Pour over the fish. Bake, uncovered, in the centre of the oven at 325 °F (170 °C), mark 3, for 25–30 minutes. Baste the mackerel 2 or 3 times with the marinade during the cooking. When cooked, allow the fish to cool at room temperature. Cover with foil and marinade in the refrigerator for at least 6 hours.

Carefully lift the fish from the liquid and transfer to a serving platter. Garnish with lemon slices and parsley.

Baked herrings with mustard sauce

4 herrings
4 oz fresh white breadcrumbs (100 g)
2 level tsps dried mixed herbs (10 ml)
2 level tsps dry mustard (10 ml)
salt and pepper
1 egg, beaten

1½ oz margarine (40 g)

For the sauce
5 oz natural yoghurt (140 g)
2 level tsps dry mustard (10 ml)

(Serves 4)

Cut off the heads and tail fins of the fish. Split them along the underside;

91

remove the entrails. Put each fish on a board cut side down and press lightly with fingers down middle of the back to loosen the bone. Turn the fish over and ease up the backbone with the fingers, removing as many small bones as possible. If the fish contains roes, remove them before filleting. Mix together the breadcrumbs, herbs, mustard, salt, pepper and egg. Insert stuffing in the herrings and place them in a shallow ovenproof dish, dot with margarine and bake, uncovered, at 375 °F (190 °C), mark 5, for about 30 minutes. Meanwhile, mix together the yoghurt and mustard and serve with the fish.

Herring fillets with onion sauce

6 oz onions, skinned and thinly sliced (150 g)
butter or margarine
2 level tbsps flour (25 g)
½ pt milk (300 ml)
½ level tsp sugar (2.5 ml)
½ level tsp dry mustard (2.5 ml)

salt and pepper
2 tbsps single cream or top of the milk (30 ml)
6 herrings, filleted
milk
2 oz fresh white breadcrumbs (50 g)
snipped chives

(Serves 6)

Sauté the onions in a covered pan in 1½ oz (40 g) fat until soft but not coloured. Stir in the flour, cook a few minutes and add the milk slowly, beating. Bring to the boil, stirring. Season with sugar, mustard, salt and pepper. Add the cream and cook for 2 minutes.

Meanwhile, rub the herring fillets with salt, dip in milk and coat in crumbs. Fry in a little hot butter or margarine until golden on both sides. Arrange overlapping on a dish, pour the sauce over and garnish with chives.

Kipper rarebit

2 fresh kippers, or 10-oz pkt frozen kipper fillets (250 g)
5 oz Cheddar cheese, grated (125 g)
knob (½ oz) butter (13 g)
3 tbsps beer or brown ale (45 ml)

1 level tsp made mustard (5 ml)
pinch cayenne pepper
salt and freshly ground black pepper
4 slices buttered toast, freshly made

(Serves 4)

Grill fresh kippers, then remove the fillets. If using frozen fillets, cook according to the directions on the packet and drain. Skin and flake the fish. Place the cheese, butter, beer, mustard and seasonings into a small pan and heat gently, stirring well until the mixture is smooth. Add the finely flaked kipper. Remove the crusts from the toast and top liberally with the kipper mixture, right to the edges. Place under a hot grill until bubbling and golden. Serve at once.

Sprats on skewers

Wash the sprats and dry them thoroughly, then toss in seasoned flour. Take some small skewers and thread 6–8 sprats on each, sticking the skewers through the heads and pushing the sprats close together. Fry in hot fat, turning them when browned on the underside. Drain on paper. Garnish with wedges of lemon.

Tuna au gratin

$\frac{1}{4}$ pint white coating sauce (125 ml)
5 oz Cheddar cheese, grated (125 g)
2 tbsps dried onion flakes (30 ml)
3 tbsps chopped parsley (45 ml)

7-oz can tuna (about 200 g)
salt and pepper
baked shortcrust pastry case,
 9 in. by 1$\frac{1}{2}$ in. deep (22.5 by 4 cm)

(Serves 6)

Make the sauce and add to it 3 oz (75 g) of the cheese, the onion flakes, parsley, and drained tuna. Season well. Pour the mixture into the pastry case, sprinkle with the remaining cheese and bake at 425 °F (220 °C), mark 7, for 10–15 minutes. Serve with a tossed green salad and jacket potatoes.

Tuna-stuffed pancakes

(see picture overleaf)

6$\frac{1}{2}$-oz can savoury tuna, drained
 (about 185 g)
2 oz margarine (50 g)
4 level tbsps plain flour (40 g)
$\frac{1}{2}$ pint milk (300 ml)
1 level tsp French mustard (5 ml)
1 tbsp lemon juice (15 ml)
salt and freshly ground black pepper

2 oz mature Cheddar cheese (50 g)
$\frac{1}{2}$ pint pancake batter (made with
 $\frac{1}{2}$ pint milk, 1 large egg, 4 oz flour,
 pinch of salt)
 (pancake batter made with 100 g plain
 flour, pinch of salt, large egg, 250 ml
 milk)
chopped parsley

(Serves 4–6)

Flake the tuna. Melt the margarine in a saucepan and stir in the flour. Cook for a few minutes. Off the heat, gradually beat in the milk then bring to the boil, stirring. Add the mustard, lemon juice, seasoning, cheese and tuna. Keep warm. Make eight 7-in. (18-cm) pancakes in the usual way. Fold the pancakes into quarters then open them out to give a pocket and fill it with tuna sauce. Arrange in a shallow dish, brush with a little more margarine and cook in the oven at 325 °F (170 °C), mark 3, for about $\frac{1}{2}$ hour. Garnish with chopped parsley.

Seafood in a cheese crust

2½ oz butter or margarine (70 g)
1½ oz lard (40 g)
7 oz plain flour (170 g)
2 oz mature Cheddar cheese,
  grated (50 g)
salt and freshly ground black pepper
pinch dry mustard

water
½ pint milk (250 ml)
1 oz capers (25 g)
7-oz can tuna, drained and flaked
  (approx. 198 g)
11½-oz can sweetcorn kernels
  (approx. 326 g)

(Serves 4–5)

Rub 1½ oz (40 g) butter and the lard into 6 oz flour. Stir in the cheese and season with salt, pepper and mustard. Mix to a soft, pliable dough with water. Knead lightly on a floured surface. Roll out three-quarters of the pastry and use to line a 2-pint (1-litre) ovenproof basin. Melt the remaining butter in a saucepan; stir in the remaining flour. Cook, stirring, for 1–2 minutes. Blend in the milk and bring to the boil, stirring. Add the capers, tuna and corn. Season to taste. Pour the sauce into the pastry-lined basin. Roll out the remaining pastry to fit the top of the basin and seal it on well. Bake in the oven at 400 °F (200 °C), mark 6, for 45 minutes. Turn out on to a warm serving dish.

Cheese and tuna quiche

4 oz shortcrust pastry
  (4 oz flour, etc.) (100 g)
1 egg
¼ pint milk (125 ml)
salt and pepper
½ medium sized onion, skinned and
  grated

3 oz Cheddar cheese, grated (75 g)
7-oz can tuna, drained and flaked
  (approx. 175 g)
parsley sprigs

(Serves 4)

Roll out the pastry and use it to line four individual 4-in. (10-cm) flan rings or one 8-in. (20-cm) ring. Whisk the egg, milk, salt and pepper, add the onion and cheese and mix well. Divide the tuna between the pastry cases and spoon the cheese custard over them. Bake in the centre of the oven at 400 °F (200 °C), mark 6, for 15 minutes. Reduce to 350 °F (180 °C), mark 4, and cook for a further 20–25 minutes until the quiches are golden brown and set. Remove the flan rings, and serve the quiches hot or cold, garnished with sprigs of parsley.

Tuna-stuffed pancakes (page 93)

9 PUDDINGS AND SWEETS

Puddings may not be nutritionally necessary but most families love them and one would have to be exceptionally penny-pinching to decide to omit them altogether. There are few more economical desserts than variations on the basic theme of baked or steamed sponge puddings or fruit pies. Steamed pudding variations – whether in flavouring, fruit, sauce, added ingredients – are endless.

But there are other interesting economical puddings, which can be adapted quite happily to use available ingredients. Canned plums or gooseberries can, for instance, replace canned rhubarb in pies, fools or other desserts. (Keep the syrup from the fruit for making into a sauce or using in a bought jelly.) Trifles and meringue sweets are not necessarily expensive. Sponge cakes, canned pineapple and custard are unlikely to be priced beyond your purse, and the cream topping doesn't have to be an inch thick; the smallest carton of cream will provide enough piped rosettes to garnish the custard covering.

Meringue nests – a delicious base for an inexpensive party sweet – are not difficult to make and the unused yolks can go into such things as lemon curd, scrambled eggs and mayonnaise. Fill the nests with fresh fruit or a pie filling, with or without fresh cream or ice cream.

Ginger pudding

4 oz self-raising flour (100 g)
1 level tbsp ground ginger (15 ml)
4 oz fresh white breadcrumbs (100 g)
4 oz shredded suet (100 g)
3 oz Demerara sugar (75 g)

2 tbsps black treacle (30 ml)
2 tbsps ginger syrup (30 ml)
2 oz stem ginger, chopped (50 g)
1 egg, beaten
6 tbsps milk (90 ml)

(Serves 6)

Half fill a large saucepan with water and put on to boil. Sift the flour and ginger together. Add all remaining ingredients and mix well together. Turn into a

-pint (1-litre) greased pudding basin, cover with greased greaseproof paper
or foil and steam for $1\frac{3}{4}$ hours. Turn out on to a warm plate and serve with
pouring custard.

Golden apple charlotte

1 lb cooking apples, peeled, cored
   and quartered (*400 g*)
2 oz golden syrup (*50 g*)
2 oz thick-cut marmalade (*50 g*)
white bread

2 oz margarine (*50 g*)
2 level tbsps granulated sugar (*30 ml*)
top of the milk or single cream,
   optional

(Serves 4)

Cut the apples into slices. Warm the syrup and marmalade in a saucepan, add
the apples and stir. Cook gently over a medium heat until the apples are soft
but not too broken up. Meanwhile, prepare $\frac{1}{2}$-in. (1-cm) slices of bread without
crusts (about 4 oz, 100 g) and cut these into even cubes. Melt the fat in a
frying pan, add the bread cubes and fry gently until evenly browned, turning
them occasionally. Stir in the sugar, turn the apple into 4 small individual
dishes, warmed, and top with fried bread cubes. If you like, drizzle the top of
each dish with top of the milk. The apple charlotte can, of course, be served
in one large dish.

Dutch apple pudding

8 oz self-raising flour (*200 g*)
$\frac{1}{2}$ level tsp salt (*2.5 ml*)
4 oz shredded suet (*100 g*)
8 tbsps water, approx. (*120 ml, approx.*)
$1\frac{3}{4}$ lb cooking apples (*700 g*)

$1\frac{1}{2}$ oz currants (*40 g*)
$1\frac{1}{2}$ oz sultanas (*40 g*)
4 oz sugar (*100 g*)
$1\frac{1}{2}$ level tbsps cornflour (*20 ml*)

(Serves 6)

Half fill a steamer or large pan with water and put it on to boil. Grease a
$2\frac{1}{2}$-pint (1.5-litre) pudding basin. Sift the flour and salt together in a basin.
Mix in the suet and bind the mixture with water to give a soft but manageable
dough. Knead the pastry lightly on a floured surface, roll it out and use two-
thirds to line the basin. Peel, core, and thickly slice the apples. Mix the remaining ingredients together and toss the apples in the sugar mixture. Pack
into the basin; top with the remaining pastry and seal well. Cover with
greaseproof paper or kitchen foil and steam for $2\frac{1}{2}$ hours. Serve with pouring
custard.

Peaches in lemon sauce

1-lb 4-oz can peach slices (566 g, approx.)
1 large egg
2 tbsps lemon juice (30 ml)

¼ pint peach syrup (150 ml)
1 level tbsp sugar (15 ml)
3-oz pkt cream cheese (75 g)

(Serves 4)

Drain the syrup from the fruit and reserve ¼ pint. Spoon the fruit into individual dessert dishes. In a double boiler, or a basin over hot water, beat together the egg, lemon juice, syrup and sugar until combined. Place over boiling water and cook until thick and smooth, stirring occasionally. Add the cream cheese and beat with a rotary whisk until smooth. Adjust the sweetness and serve warm – not hot – or cool, over the peach slices.

Orange syrup sponge

4 tbsps golden syrup (60 ml)
3 medium sized oranges
4 oz margarine (100 g)

4 oz caster sugar (100 g)
2 eggs, beaten
4 oz self-raising flour, sifted (100 g)

(Serves 6)

Half fill a large saucepan with water and put on to boil. Grease a 2-pint (1-litre) pudding basin. Spoon the golden syrup into the base. Grate the rind from 1 orange, squeeze it and keep the juice. Slice the two remaining oranges thinly. Press the orange slices on to the base and sides of the basin. Cream together the margarine and sugar until light and creamy. Add the beaten eggs a little at a time with the rind and juice; finally fold in the flour. Spoon the mixture into the basin, cover with buttered greaseproof paper or foil, secure tightly. Steam for about 1½ hours. Unmould and serve with warm syrup if wished.

Black cap pudding
(see picture opposite)

3 oz mixed dried fruit (75 g)
1½ oz Demerara sugar (40 g)
½ oz butter or margarine, melted (about 15 g)
4 oz margarine (100 g)

4 oz caster sugar (100 g)
grated rind of ½ lemon
2 eggs, beaten
6 oz self-raising flour (150 g)
little milk to mix

(Serves 4–6)

Half fill a large saucepan with water and put on to boil. Grease a 2-pint

Black cap pudding

(1-litre) pudding basin. Combine the dried fruit, Demerara sugar and melted butter or margarine. Use this mixture to line the base of the pudding basin. Cream 4 oz margarine, the sugar and lemon rind together until pale and fluffy. Gradually add the eggs, beating well after each addition. Fold in the sifted flour with a metal spoon and add enough milk – about 1 tbsp (15 ml) – to give a dropping consistency. Place the mixture in the basin, cover with greased greaseproof paper or foil and steam for about 1½ hours. Turn out and serve with custard or cream.

Steamed chocolate pudding

2 oz plain chocolate (*50 g*)
1 level tbsp cocoa (*15 ml*)
6 tbsps milk (*100 ml*)
2 oz fresh white breadcrumbs (*50 g*)
4 oz margarine (*100 g*)

4 oz caster sugar (*100 g*)
2 eggs
4 oz self-raising flour (*100 g*)
chocolate sauce (see below)

(Serves 4–6)

Half fill a large saucepan with water and put to boil. Grease a 2-pint (1.5-litre) pudding basin. Melt the chocolate in a basin over hot water. Blend the cocoa with 1 tbsp (15 ml) milk and soak the breadcrumbs in the remaining milk. Cream the fat and sugar until pale and fluffy; beat in the eggs and flour together. Fold through the chocolate, cocoa and crumbs. Spoon the mixture into the pudding basin. Slightly hollow the centre and cover with greased greaseproof paper or foil. Steam for about 2 hours. To serve, turn out and pour a little sauce over the pudding. Serve the rest of the sauce separately.

Chocolate sauce
Blend 1 level tbsp (15 ml) cornflour and 1 level tbsp (15 ml) cocoa with a little cold milk taken from ½ pint (250 ml). Heat remaining milk, pour on to the cocoa, return to pan and reheat, stirring.

Lemon syrup layer

8 oz self-raising flour (*200 g*)
½ level tsp salt (*2.5 ml*)
4 oz white vegetable fat (*100 g*)
5 tbsps water (*75 ml*)

grated rind of 1 lemon
1½ tbsps lemon juice (*20 ml*)
12 oz golden syrup (*300 g*)
2 oz fresh white breadcrumbs (*50 g*)

(Serves 4)

Sift together the flour and salt into a bowl. Rub in the fat, add the grated rind and water and with a round-bladed knife knit together to a soft manageable dough. Knead lightly on a floured surface.

Grease a 1-pint (600 ml) pudding basin. Divide the pastry into four. Combine the lemon juice, golden syrup and breadcrumbs and place a little in the base of the basin. Roll out one piece of the pastry to fit the base, put into the basin and cover with more syrup filling. Repeat the layers of pastry and syrup, ending with pastry. Cover with foil or double greaseproof paper and steam for 2 hours; turn out and serve piping hot.

Frosted gooseberry plate pie
(see picture page 103)

8 oz self-raising flour (200 g)
pinch of salt
2 oz lard (50 g)
2 oz margarine (50 g)
1 oz caster sugar (25 g)
1 egg, separated

water
1 lb gooseberries (400 g)
3 oz sugar (75 g)
2 level tbsps flour (30 ml)
grated rind of 1 orange
2 oz icing sugar (50 g)

(Serves 4–6)

Combine the flour and salt in a bowl. Rub in the fats and add the sugar. Blend the egg yolk with 4 tsps (20 ml) water; stir it into the flour with more water to give a manageable dough. Divide in half, roll out one portion and use it to line an 8-in. (20-cm) pie plate, preferably metal. Top and tail the gooseberries, cutting a small slice from the end. Mix the sugar, flour and orange rind and sprinkle over the fruit. Roll out the remaining pastry and use for a lid. Make a slit in the lid. Bake in the oven at 400 °F (200 °C), mark 6, for about 45 minutes. Brush the pie with frosting, made by blending together the egg white and icing sugar, then return it to the oven for 5 minutes. Serve warm or cold.

Banana-apricot fool

1-lb 13-oz can apricot halves (822 g)
½ lb bananas, peeled (200 g)
2 tbsps lemon juice (30 ml)

1 level tsp powdered gelatine (5 ml)
2 tbsps juice from apricots (30 ml)
small can evaporated milk, chilled

(Serves 4–6)

Place the drained apricots with the bananas in a blender. Add the lemon juice and blend until smooth (or press through a sieve). Turn the purée into a bowl. Dissolve the gelatine in 2 tbsps juice from the apricots, in a bowl over a pan of hot water, then stir it into the apricots. Whisk the evaporated milk until really thick and fold into the fruit mixture. Divide between 4–6 stemmed glasses. Chill for 1 hour before serving.

Syrup creams

1½ level tbsps powdered gelatine (*20 ml*)
3 tbsps water (*45 ml*)
2 oz golden syrup (*50 g*)
2 oz black treacle (*50 g*)
1½ pints milk (*750 ml*)

(Serves 6)

Dissolve the gelatine in the water, in a small basin placed over a pan of hot water. In another bowl, blend the syrup and treacle with a little of the milk. Add the remaining milk. When the gelatine is lukewarm, stir in a little of the syrup and return this to the bulk. Divide between six glasses and chill.

Junket

1 pint rich milk (*500 ml*)
½–1 oz caster sugar (*15–25 g*)
1 tsp rennet (*5 ml*)
nutmeg, cinnamon sugar or chocolate, to decorate
vanilla essence, optional

(Serves 4)

Warm the milk to blood heat, stirring in the sugar until dissolved. Remove from the heat, stir in the rennet and pour the mixture immediately into a serving dish or individual dishes. Leave at room temperature until set.

Grate nutmeg over the junket just before serving with farm-fresh clotted cream, or serve cinnamon sugar or grated chocolate on the side. Alternatively add a little vanilla essence to the milk before stirring in the rennet.

Pears in orange-caramel sauce

(*see picture opposite*)

4 even sized dessert pears
4 oz granulated sugar (*100 g*)
1 large juicy orange
2 level tsps arrowroot (*10 ml*)
knob of butter or margarine
long shred coconut (optional)

(Serves 4)

Halve the pears, scoop out the core, peel them and discard the stems. Place the pear halves, hollow side up, in a deep frying pan. Add 3 oz (75 g) sugar, the pared rind of the orange and enough water just to cover. Bring to the boil, reduce the heat and cook until the pears are soft but not mushy and slightly transparent. Lift out the pears and place them in a serving dish.

Reduce the liquid in the pan to ¼ pint (150 ml) by boiling. In a small pan, dissolve the rest of the sugar, shaking the pan occasionally, then heat until it caramelises. Off the heat, pour in the strained pear liquor and the orange

Frosted gooseberry plate pie (*page 101*), pears in orange-caramel sauce

juice; stir to dissolve caramel. Blend the arrowroot to a cream with a little water and add to the juices with the butter or margarine, stirring. Cook until clear. Spoon over the pears and chill. Decorate with long shred coconut (optional).

Apple whip

large can evaporated milk, chilled
1 pint apple purée (*500 ml*)
pinch of ground cloves

pinch of ground coriander
finely grated rind of 1 lemon

(Serves 4–6)

Whip the milk until thick and doubled in volume. Blend in the purée, spices and lemon rind. Pour into a serving dish or individual glasses.

Meringue shells

3 egg whites (the yolks can be
incorporated in the filling)

6 oz caster sugar (*150 g*)

Draw some 3-in. (7.5-cm) circles on a sheet of silicone (non-stick) paper and place the paper on a baking sheet. Whisk the egg whites until stiff, whisk in half the sugar until stiff, then fold in the remaining sugar. Spread some of the meringue over the circles to form bases and, with a large star vegetable nozzle, pipe the remainder to form the edges (or make a rim with the help of a spoon). Bake towards the bottom of the oven at 250 °F (130 °C), mark $\frac{1}{4}$–$\frac{1}{2}$, for $1\frac{1}{2}$–2 hours, or until dry. Leave to cool on a rack, remove the paper and fill (see below).

Fillings for meringue cases
1. Fresh fruit mixed with whipped sweetened cream.
2. Canned fruit, jam-glazed.
3. Orange filling: Grate the rind from 1 orange and squeeze out the juice. Squeeze the juice from a lemon. Mix the rinds and juices and make up to $\frac{1}{2}$ pint (250 ml) with water. Blend 2 level tbsps (30 ml) custard powder and 1 level tbsp (15 ml) sugar with a little of the juice, heat the rest, and pour it on to the blended mixture, then return it to the pan, stirring over gentle heat until it thickens. Cool slightly and add 2 of the egg yolks left from the meringue mixture.
4. Lemon filling: Make up a packet of lemon pie filling, using slightly less water than usual, and fold in 2 egg yolks. (This is a very quickly made filling.)

10 CAKES AND COOKIES

Cutting out cakes and cookies is one way of saving money on food – but not the most agreeable. However, making your own cakes, as opposed to buying them, *is* money-saving. Deliciousness is not related to the amount you spend on the ingredients. Try some of the ideas in this chapter to prove the point; they include some continuingly popular old family favourites.

Gingerbread

8 oz plain flour (*200 g*)
½ level tsp salt (*2.5 ml*)
1½ level tsps ground ginger (*7.5 ml*)
1½ level tsps baking powder (*7.5 ml*)
½ level tsp bicarbonate of soda (*2.5 ml*)
4 oz Demerara sugar (*100 g*)

3 oz margarine (*75 g*)
3 oz black treacle (*75 g*)
3 oz golden syrup (*75 g*)
¼ pint milk (*150 ml*)
1 small egg

Grease and line a 7-in. (18-cm) square cake tin. Sift together the flour, salt, ginger, baking powder and bicarbonate of soda. Warm the sugar, margarine, treacle and syrup to melt the margarine but do not overheat. Stir the warm syrup into the dry ingredients with the milk and beaten egg. Beat well. Pour into the tin and bake in the centre of the oven at 350 °F (180 °C), mark 4, for about 1 hour, until well risen and firm to the touch. Turn out and cool on a wire rack.

Grandmother's boiled fruit cake

½ pint tea (*250 ml*)
4 oz margarine (*100 g*)
5 oz light soft brown sugar (*125 g*)
6 oz currants (*150 g*)
6 oz sultanas (*150 g*)

3 level tsps mixed spice (*15 ml*)
10 oz plain flour (*250 g*)
2 level tsps bicarbonate of soda (*10 ml*)
1 large egg, beaten

Grease a 7-in. (18-cm) round cake tin. Put the tea, margarine, sugar, currants, sultanas and spice into a saucepan. Bring to the boil. Reduce the heat and simmer for 20 minutes. Cool. Lightly beat in the sifted flour and bicarbonate of soda with the egg. Turn the mixture into the tin and bake just below the centre of the oven for about 1 hour at 350 °F (180 °C), mark 4. When the cake is beginning to brown, cover with a piece of greaseproof paper. Turn out and cool on a wire rack.

Cherry and raisin cake
(see picture opposite)

12 oz self-raising flour (300 g)
pinch of salt
6 oz margarine (150 g)
6 oz glacé cherries (150 g)
4 oz stoned raisins (100 g)

2 oz desiccated coconut (50 g)
6 oz caster sugar (150 g)
2 large eggs
$\frac{1}{4}$ pint milk, approx. (150 ml, approx.)

Grease a $7\frac{1}{2}$–8 in. (18–20 cm) round cake tin. Sift the flour and salt into a bowl. Rub in the fat until the mixture resembles fine breadcrumbs. Halve the cherries and raisins, using scissors, toss them in the coconut and add to the dry ingredients with the caster sugar. Stir to combine. Whisk the eggs and milk together and stir into the bowl to mix well. Beat the mixture lightly. Turn it into the prepared tin and level the surface. Bake in the centre of the oven at 350 °F (180 °C), mark 4, for about $1\frac{1}{2}$ hours, until well risen and golden brown. Leave in the tin for 15 minutes before turning out on to a wire rack to cool.

Tutti frutti layer cake
(see picture page 111)

6 oz margarine (150 g)
    or 3 oz butter and 3 oz margarine
    (or 75 g and 75 g)
6 oz caster sugar (150 g)
3 eggs, beaten
6 oz self-raising flour (150 g)
grated rind of 1 lemon
$\frac{1}{2}$ oz angelica (approx. 10 g)

1 oz glacé cherries (25 g)
$\frac{1}{2}$ oz flaked almonds (approx. 10 g)

For the filling
$1\frac{1}{2}$ oz margarine (40 g)
3 oz icing sugar (75 g)
1 tbsp lemon juice (15 ml)

Grease and line the bases of two 8-in. (20-cm) straight sided sandwich tins. Cream the fat, add the sugar and beat until light and fluffy. Beat in the eggs, a little at a time. Lightly beat in the flour together with the lemon rind. Divide equally between the tins and level the surfaces. Scissor-snip the angelica and the cherries into small pieces and scatter with the almonds over the surface of one cake. Bake just above the oven centre at 350 °F (180 °C), mark 4, for about 25 minutes or until spongy to the touch. Turn out and cool

Chocolate fudge cake (*page 110*), Vienna fingers (*page 112*),
apple and walnut teabread (*page 113*), cherry and raisin
cake (*above*)

on a wire rack. For the filling, cream the margarine and gradually beat in the icing sugar and lemon juice.

Coffee marble cake
(*see picture page 110*)

8 oz margarine (*200 g*)
8 oz caster sugar (*200 g*)
4 large eggs

8 oz self-raising flour (*200 g*)
2 tbsps coffee essence (*30 ml*)
icing sugar

Grease a 3½-pint (2-litre) fluted or plain ring mould. Beat the fat until soft but not oily. Add the sugar and cream until light and fluffy. Add the eggs one at a time, beating between each addition. Lightly beat in the sifted flour. Divide the mixture into two parts; to one part add the coffee essence. Place the mixtures in alternate spoonfuls into the prepared tin. Level the surface and swirl through the mixture with a skewer; don't overdo the movement, or the effect will be disappointing. Bake in the centre of the oven at 350°F (180°C), mark 4, for about 45 minutes, until well risen and spongy to the touch. Turn out on to a wire rack to cool. Serve dusted with icing sugar.

Economical Christmas cake

8 oz sultanas (*200 g*)
4 oz currants (*100 g*)
8 oz stoned raisins (*200 g*)
10 oz plain flour (*250 g*)
1 level tsp mixed spice (*5 ml*)
a little grated nutmeg
8 oz margarine (*200 g*)
8 oz caster sugar (*200 g*)

a little grated lemon rind
few drops almond essence
4 eggs, beaten
1 level tbsp marmalade (*15 ml*)
½ level tsp bicarbonate of soda (*2.5 ml*)
2 tbsps milk or water (*30 ml*)
few drops gravy browning

Line an 8-in. (20-cm) cake tin, using a double thickness of greaseproof paper. Mix the fruit, flour, spice and nutmeg. Cream the fat, sugar, lemon rind and essence together until pale and fluffy. Add the eggs a little at a time, beating well after each addition; add the marmalade and mix thoroughly. Fold in half the flour and fruit, using a metal spoon, then fold in the rest. Dissolve the bicarbonate of soda in the milk or water and stir into the mixture with a few drops of gravy browning; the mixture should be of a soft dropping consistency. Put into the tin and bake towards the bottom of the oven at 300°F (150°C), mark 1–2, for about 4 hours. Cool in the tin and then turn out on to a wire rack. Wrap in several layers of greaseproof paper before putting in an airtight tin to store. Or cover the wrapped cake entirely in aluminium foil.

Honey butter sandwich

4 oz margarine (100 g)
4 oz caster sugar (100 g)
2 large eggs
4 oz self-raising flour (100 g)
½ level tsp ground cinnamon (2.5 ml)

For the frosting
3 oz butter (75 g)

6 oz icing sugar, sifted (150 g)
1 level tbsp clear honey (15 ml)
1 tbsp lemon juice (15 ml)
icing sugar for dusting

Grease and line the bases of two 7-in. (18-cm) straight sided sandwich tins. Cream the fat and sugar, beat in the eggs one at a time and lightly beat in the flour and cinnamon, sifted together. Divide the mixture equally between prepared tins and bake in the centre of the oven at 350 °F (180 °C), mark 4, for 25 minutes, until well risen and spongy to the touch. Turn out and cool on a wire rack.

Meanwhile, cream the butter for the frosting and gradually beat in the icing sugar with the honey and lemon juice. Layer the cakes with half the filling, top with the remainder and swirl it with a knife. Dust with icing sugar.

Genoese sponge

3 eggs
4 oz caster sugar (100 g)
3 oz plain flour (75 g)
3 tbsps cooking oil (45 ml)

American frosting
8 oz granulated sugar (200 g)
4 tbsps water (60 ml)
1 egg white

Grease and line the bases of two 6-in. (15-cm) sandwich tins. Put the eggs and sugar in a large bowl, stand this over a pan of hot water and whisk until light and creamy; when ready, the mixture should be stiff enough to hold an impression of the whisk for a few seconds. Remove from the heat and whisk until cool. Lightly fold in the flour alternately with the oil. Pour the mixture into the tins and bake towards the top of the oven at 375 °F (190 °C), mark 5, until golden-brown and firm to the touch.

When cold, sandwich the sponges together with jam and decorate either with butter icing or with American frosting (see below).

To make the frosting:

Gently heat the sugar in the water, stirring until dissolved. Then continue to heat *without stirring* to 240 °F (116 °C). Beat the egg white until stiff. Remove the sugar syrup from the heat and, when the bubbles subside, pour it on to the egg white. Beat the mixture continuously as it cools. When thick and nearly cold, pour the frosting quickly over the cake.

Chocolate fudge cake

(see picture page 107)

3 oz margarine *(75 g)*
3 oz caster sugar *(75 g)*
1 large egg
2 oz golden syrup *(50 g)*
5 oz plain flour *(125 g)*
1 oz cocoa *(25 g)*
½ level tsp bicarbonate of soda *(2.5 ml)*
2 level tsps baking powder *(10 ml)*
few drops vanilla essence
¼ pint buttermilk *(150 ml)*

For the frosting
2 oz plain chocolate *(50 g)*
3 tbsps water *(45 ml)*
1 oz margarine *(25 g)*
7 oz icing sugar, sifted *(175 g)*

Cream together the fat and sugar until light and fluffy. Beat in the egg and syrup. Sift together the flour, cocoa, bicarbonate of soda and baking powder and add to the creamed mixture alternately with the essence and buttermilk; beat lightly. Turn into a greased and lined 7–7½ in. (17–18 cm) deep sandwich tin, or a tin with the sides raised with a greaseproof paper collar to give a total depth of about 2 in. (5 cm). Bake in the centre of the oven at 375 °F (190 °C), mark 5, for about 30 minutes. Turn out and cool on a wire rack.

Coffee marble cake *(page 108)*.

110

Tutti frutti layer cake *(page 111)*.

Fix a band of greaseproof paper round the cake to come bout $\frac{3}{4}$–1 in. (2 cm) above the highest part of the cake. Secure with a paperclip. Spoon frosting (see below) over the top when beginning to set, and swirl with a knife. Leave until firm, but not hard, before cutting.

To make the frosting: In a small pan, melt the chocolate with water; do not boil. Off the heat, add the margarine in small pieces. When melted, gradually beat in the icing sugar.

Melting moments

4 oz margarine (*100 g*)
3 oz sugar (*75 g*)
1 egg yolk

few drops vanilla essence
5 oz self-raising flour (*125 g*)
crushed cornflakes

(Makes 20–24)

Grease 2 baking trays. Cream the margarine and sugar together and beat in the egg yolk. Flavour with vanilla essence, stir in the flour to give a stiff dough and divide into 20–24 portions. Form each into a ball and roll them in crushed cornflakes. Place on the baking trays and bake for 15–20 minutes at 375 °F (190 °C), mark 5. Cool on the trays for a few minutes before lifting on to a wire rack.

Vienna fingers
(*see picture page 107*)

4 oz margarine (*100 g*)
3 oz caster sugar (*75 g*)
1 egg
grated rind of 1 lemon
6 oz plain flour (*150 g*)
1 level tsp baking powder (*5 ml*)
apricot jam

For the lemon icing
3 oz icing sugar, sifted (*75 g*)
lemon juice

Cream the margarine until soft. Add the sugar and beat until light and fluffy. Beat in the egg and lemon rind. Sift in the flour and baking powder, stirring until combined. Chill the dough for about 30 minutes until of a manageable consistency, then knead lightly. On a floured surface, shape into two equal pieces and roll into 'ropes' about 12 in. (30 cm) long. Keeping them the same length, press out to about 2 in. (5 cm) wide. Lift on to greased baking sheets, using a palette knife. With the back of a knife make a slight indentation down the length in the centres. Fill this with firm jam. Bake in the centre of the oven at 400 °F (200 °C), mark 6, for about 15 minutes, until risen and golden-brown. Remove from the oven and, while still hot, brush with lemon glacé icing; add more jam. Cool. Serve in slices – eat fresh.

To make the icing: blend the icing sugar in a small bowl with enough lemon juice to give a thick coating consistency.

Cornish fairings

4 oz plain flour (*100 g*)
pinch salt
1 level tsp baking powder (*5 ml*)
1 level tsp bicarbonate of soda (*5 ml*)
1 level tsp ground ginger (*5 ml*)

½ level tsp mixed spice (*2.5 ml*)
2 oz margarine (*50 g*)
2 oz sugar (*50 g*)
3 level tbsps golden syrup (*45 ml*)

Grease 2 baking trays. Sift the flour with the salt, baking powder and other dry ingredients. Rub in the margarine and add the sugar. Warm the syrup and add to the other ingredients; mix well to a fairly stiff consistency. Roll into small balls and place them 4 in. (10 cm) apart on the baking trays. Bake fairly near the top of the oven at 400 °F (200 °C), mark 6, for 5 minutes, then move them to a lower shelf and continue cooking for a further 5–8 minutes. Lift on to a wire rack to cool.

Apple and walnut teabread
(*see picture page 107*)

4 oz margarine (*100 g*)
4 oz caster sugar (*100 g*)
2 large eggs
1 level tbsp honey or golden
   syrup (*15 ml*)
4 oz sultanas (*100 g*)
2 oz shelled walnuts, chopped (*50 g*)

8 oz self-raising flour (*200 g*)
salt
1 level tsp mixed spice (*5 ml*)
1 medium cooking apple, peeled, cored
   and chopped
icing sugar

The fat should be at room temperature. In a large, deep bowl place all the ingredients except the icing sugar and beat with a wooden spoon until well combined – about 2 minutes. Turn into a greased and lined loaf tin about 8½ in. by 4½ in. (20 cm by 10 cm), top measurements, by 2½ in. (6 cm) deep. Level the surface. Bake in the centre of the oven at 350 °F (180 °C), mark 4, for 1 hour. Reduce the oven temperature to 325 °F (170 °C), mark 3, for about a further 20 minutes. Turn out and cool on a wire rack. When cold, dredge with icing sugar. Serve thickly sliced and buttered.

Shortbread

5 oz plain flour (*125 g*)
1 oz rice flour (*25 g*)
2 oz caster sugar (*50 g*)

4 oz butter or margarine or half and
   half (*100 g*)

Grease a baking tray. Sift the flours and add the sugar. Knead in the fat;

keep it in one piece and gradually work in the dry ingredients. Knead well and pack into two well floured $\frac{1}{4}$-pint (150-ml) wooden shortbread moulds, or a 7-in. (18-cm) sandwich tin. Turn out on to the baking tray and prick well. Bake at 300 °F (150 °C), mark 2, until firm and golden — about 1 hour. Turn out and dredge with sugar. Serve cut into fingers.

Note: the rice flour is a traditional ingredient, but it can be omitted; in this case, use 6 oz (150 g) plain flour.

Date and raisin crunch

2 oz stoned dates *(50 g)*
1 oz seedless raisins *(25 g)*
juice and grated rind of 1 orange
4 oz rolled oats *(100 g)*

1½ oz plain flour *(40 g)*
3 oz margarine *(75 g)*
1½ oz sugar *(40 g)*

Scissor-snip the dates into a small pan and add the raisins. Make the juice of the orange up to $\frac{1}{4}$ pint (150 ml) with water; add to the pan and cook gently until the mixture is thick. Cool.

Mix the oats and flour in a bowl and rub in the margarine. Add the sugar and grated orange rind. Press half into a 7-in. (18-cm) spring-release or loose-bottomed sandwich tin. Spread the filling over and sprinkle the rest of the oat crumble on top. Press down lightly with a round bladed knife and bake in the oven at 375 °F (190 °C), mark 5, for 40 minutes. Turn out and cool on a wire rack.

11 SLIMMERS' MEALS FOR SLIM BUDGETS

A slimming routine doesn't necessarily call for a diet of grilled steak and fresh pineapple. It is possible to save money even when you are having to cut down on the cheaper carbohydrates that would form part of your normal diet. If you are slimming and also have to feed a family of normal eaters at the same time, you will want to try and cater for everyone simultaneously, and this can be done. The slimmer need not eat the extra fattening carbohydrates which the rest of the family can eat in pastries, puddings and potatoes, for instance; and you can make casseroles for everyone from cheaper cuts of meat, offal and fish.

Use more of the cheaper protein foods such as eggs, milk and cheese, and make full use of fresh vegetables and fruit in season to add bulk to a diet-on-a-budget. Don't leave out potatoes completely as they provide essential nourishment; but don't have more than a small helping once a day. You can also use the economically priced pulses, in moderation, to give extra food value. Use dried skimmed milk in cooking to cut the proportion of fat in your diet.

An interesting salad which can provide you with a main meal, can double as an accompaniment to some 'forbidden' food which the family are having, to save you working out two different mealtime ideas.

Baked mackerel
(*see picture page 117*)

4 mackerel, cleaned and heads removed
2 shallots, skinned and finely sliced
4 medium-sized tomatoes, skinned

4 oz mushrooms, sliced (*100 g*)
juice of 1 lemon
lemon and dill for garnish

(Serves 4)

Lightly oil 4 sheets of foil; place 1 mackerel on each sheet and add some of the shallots, tomatoes, mushrooms and lemon juice. Parcel up the foil, place the fish on a baking sheet and bake at 350 °F (180 °C), mark 4, for about 30 minutes. Remove the foil and garnish with slices of lemon and dill.

Simple fish curry

1 lb filleted white fish (*400 g*)
2 level tsps curry powder (*10 ml*)
salt and pepper
1 tbsp cooking oil (*15 ml*)

2 onions, skinned and chopped
3 tomatoes, skinned and sliced
parsley, to garnish

(Serves 3)

Cut the fish into serving portions. Mix together the seasonings and rub into the fish. Heat the oil and fry the fish lightly. Add the remaining ingredients, cover and cook over a low heat for 10–15 minutes until the fish is flaky but firm. Garnish with parsley.

Slimmers can't go wrong with salads

Baked mackerel (*page 115*)

Curried eggs

2 eggs, hardboiled
1 oz margarine (*25 g*)
1 small onion, skinned and chopped
small piece of apple, finely chopped
½ level tsp curry powder (*2.5 ml*)
½ oz flour (*10 ml*)

¼ pint stock (*125 ml*)
salt
1 tsp lemon juice (*5 ml*)
2 oz cooked long grain rice (*50 g*)
lemon to garnish

(Serves 1)

While the boiled eggs are still hot, cut one of them into small pieces and the other into wedges. Melt the margarine, fry the onion lightly, add the apple, curry powder and flour and cook for a few minutes. Gradually add the stock, salt and lemon juice. Boil up and skim, then simmer this sauce for about 15 minutes. Add the cut-up egg to the sauce and when heated through place in a hot dish surrounded by rice. Decorate with wedges of egg and lemon.

Baked eggs and mushrooms

½ lb mushrooms (*200 g*)
2 tbsps cooking oil (*30 ml*)
4–6 eggs

salt and pepper
2 oz Cheshire or Cheddar cheese,
   grated (*50 g*)

(Serves 4)

Wipe and thinly slice the mushrooms. Fry in the oil and put into a shallow heatproof dish. Break the required number of eggs into the dish, season and sprinkle with grated cheese. Bake in the oven at 350 °F (180 °C), mark 4, until the eggs have just set.

Bengal chicken curry

(*see picture page 121*)

1 tbsp cooking oil (*15 ml*)
2 onions, skinned and chopped
1 clove garlic, skinned and crushed
1 level tsp dry mustard (*5 ml*)
1 level tsp curry powder (*5 ml*)

4 chicken joints
½ pint chicken stock (*250 ml*)
2 level tbsps tomato paste (*30 ml*)
salt and pepper

(Serves 4)

Heat the oil and sauté the onions and garlic. Mix together the mustard and curry powder and rub it into the chicken joints. Add the joints to the pan and brown lightly. Mix together the stock and tomato paste, pour over the chicken and add a little salt and pepper. Cover and bake at 350 °F (180 °C), mark 5, for 1 hour.

Sausage casserole

1½ lb beef sausages (*600 g*)
½ lb carrots, peeled and grated (*200 g*)
3 onions, skinned and finely chopped
2 apples, peeled, cored and sliced
2 level tbsps flour (*30 ml*)
salt and pepper

2 tbsps vinegar (*30 ml*)
1 tsp Worcestershire sauce (*5 ml*)
11-oz can tomato juice (*about 300 g*)
¼ pint water (*125 ml*)
artificial sweetener to taste

(Serves 4)

Prick the sausages and cover with hot water; bring to the boil, boil for 10 minutes and pour off the liquid. Skin the sausages under cold water and drain again. Cut the meat into pieces and place in a casserole with the prepared vegetables and apples. Mix together the flour, salt, pepper, vinegar, sauce, tomato juice and water. Pour this over the sausage and vegetable mixture, cover and cook at 350 °F (180 °C), mark 4, for 1 hour. Adjust the sharpness by adding sweetener to taste.

Liver and bacon casserole

1 lb liver (*450 g*)
seasoned flour
a little cooking oil or dripping
1 onion, skinned and chopped
1 carrot, peeled and sliced

1–2 tomatoes, skinned and roughly
   chopped
3–4 bacon rashers, rinded and cut into
   short lengths

(Serves 4)

Cut the liver into small chunks, toss in the seasoned flour and fry in hot oil or dripping. Add the onion, carrot and tomatoes. Barely cover with water, then bring to the boil, stirring. Put into a casserole and cook in the oven at 350 °F (180 °C), mark 4, for about 45 minutes, or until tender. Cover the top with the cut-up bacon rashers and replace in the oven until the bacon is browned – about 20 minutes.

Pork and liver loaf
(*see picture page 124*)

1 lb lean pork (*400 g*)
½ lb lamb's liver (*200 g*)
1 onion, skinned
2 oz soft breadcrumbs (*50 g*)

1 level tsp dried thyme (*5 ml*)
1 egg, lightly beaten
salt and pepper

(Serves 4)

Mince together the pork, liver and onion. Blend in the breadcrumbs and thyme and bind with seasoned egg. Shape into an oblong and wrap firmly in foil. Place in a greased baking dish (about 7½ in. by 5 in., 18 cm by 12 cm) and bake at 350 °F (180 °C), mark 4, for 1½ hours. Serve with apple sauce.

Minted breast of lamb

2 breasts of lamb, boned
2 large cooking apples, peeled
2 tbsps chopped mint (*30 ml*)

1 oz fresh white breadcrumbs (*25 g*)
salt and pepper

(Serves 4)

Trim the breasts of lamb, removing excess fat. Coarsely grate the apple and mix with the mint and breadcrumbs. Spread this stuffing over each breast, roll up tightly and secure with skewers or string. Season, put in a shallow baking dish and bake, uncovered, at 350 °F (180 °C), mark 4, for about 1½ hours.

Russian casseroled beefsteak

1½ lb braising steak (650 g)
1 oz plain flour (25 g)
oil for frying
2 raw potatoes, peeled and thinly sliced

6 small cabbage leaves
2 carrots, peeled and sliced
6 peppercorns
3 tomatoes, skinned and sliced
stock or water if required

(Serves 4)

Wipe the steak and beat well, then cut it into 4-in. (10-cm) squares. Coat with flour and fry in the oil until browned. Put into a deep casserole layers of steak, potato, whole cabbage leaves and sliced carrot, with the peppercorns and tomatoes. Cover and bake at 350 °F (180 °C), mark 4, for about 2 hours. Add 1 tbsp (15 ml) stock or water during cooking if necessary – but the juice from the meat and vegetables may give enough liquid; the casserole should be kept fairly dry.

Stuffed cabbage leaves
(see picture page 128)

¼–¾ lb minced raw meat (200–300 g)
1 onion, skinned and chopped
1 tbsp cooking oil (15 ml)
2 tsps chopped parsley (10 ml)

salt and pepper
stock
2 tbsps cooked long grain rice (30 ml)
8–12 medium sized cabbage leaves

(Serves 4)

Cook the minced meat and chopped onion in the hot oil, turning the mixture frequently. Add parsley, salt and a little stock and simmer for 10 minutes, then stir in the rice. Break off the cabbage leaves, remove the hard white spine, blanch the leaves in boiling water for 2 minutes and drain them. Place 1 tbsp of the meat mixture on each leaf and fold it over the filling to make a neat parcel. Put the parcels close together in a casserole, almost cover with stock, cover and cook in the oven at 350 °F (180 °C), mark 4, for about 45 minutes.

Bengal chicken curry (page 118)

Finnish cabbage and lamb hot-pot

2 lb white cabbage (*1 kg*)
1 lb best end of neck of lamb (*500 g*)

salt and pepper
tomato paste to taste

(Serves 4)

Wash the cabbage and chop it finely. Brown the meat on both sides in a saucepan without any extra fat, then add the cabbage, seasoning, tomato paste and a very little water and simmer until the cabbage is quite transparent and the meat tender.

Marrow and tomato bake

½ a vegetable marrow, cubed
salt and pepper
½ lb tomatoes (*200 g*)
½ pint cheese sauce (*250 ml*)

toast triangles (use starch-reduced
  bread)
parsley to garnish

(Serves 3–4)

Grease a casserole and put in the marrow, with salt and pepper. Cover and cook gently at 350 °F (180 °C), mark 4, until the marrow is almost tender. Add the skinned and quartered tomatoes and the cheese sauce. Leave the lid off to brown the top and serve with the toast triangles and parsley garnish.

Scrambled bacon and corn

1 oz butter or margarine (*25 g*)
1 medium sized onion, finely chopped
3 oz bacon, chopped (*75 g*)
11-oz can whole-kernel corn (*about*
  300 g)

4 eggs
salt and pepper
Worcestershire sauce
parsley

(Serves 4)

Melt the butter and fry the onion and bacon until golden; add the corn. Beat the eggs, season well and add with a little Worcestershire sauce to the pan. Stir and heat slowly until the egg is cooked; garnish with parsley.

Dressings for salads

Cheese dressing

4 oz cottage cheese (*100 g*)
juice of ½ lemon

salt and pepper

Combine the ingredients and sieve or blend until smooth and creamy. Adjust the seasoning. If the lemon is very acid, add 1–2 drops liquid sweetener.

Garlic dressing

2 pimientos (a 3¼-oz can) (*80 g approx*)
2 tbsps salad oil (*30 ml*)
2 tbsps white vinegar (*30 ml*)

1 clove garlic, skinned and crushed
salt and pepper

Sieve or blend the pimientos. Beat in the oil, vinegar and garlic. Season to taste.

Lemon dressing

Mix together 1 tsp (5 ml) soy sauce and the juice of 1 lemon, with liquid sweetener to taste.

Lemon chive dressing

8 oz cottage cheese (*200 g*)
1 tbsp lemon juice (*15 ml*)
1 tbsp salad oil (*15 ml*)

salt and pepper
1 tbsp chopped chives (*15 ml*)

Sieve or blend the cheese, then add remaining ingredients. Chill before serving.

Cheddar cheese salad

4 oz Cheddar cheese (*100 g*)
½ lb tomatoes, skinned and thinly sliced (*200 g*)
mayonnaise

a little made mustard
a lettuce
watercress
chopped chives

Cut the cheese into very small cubes and mix with the tomatoes, mayonnaise and mustard. Make a bed of torn lettuce leaves and watercress sprigs, put the cheese and tomato on top and sprinkle with the chopped chives.

Cole slaw bowl

1 large round cabbage
4 raw carrots, peeled and grated
1 spring onion, trimmed and chopped
2 oz Cheddar cheese, grated (50 g)

1 tbsp chopped chives (15 ml)
salt and pepper
mayonnaise
1 tomato, skinned, seeded and sliced

Remove any tough outside leaves from the cabbage, then hollow it out with a sharp knife to make a 'bowl'. Slice the inside of the cabbage, removing the coarse ribs, and mix with the carrot, onion, cheese and chives. Season well. Add a little mayonnaise to bind it together and pile the mixture back into the cabbage. Garnish with the tomato.

Hot slaw salad

2 lb cabbage, cooked (1 kg)
2 tbsps vinegar (30 ml)
salt
a little dry mustard
liquid sweetener

3 eggs
½ pint milk (250 ml)
2 rashers of back bacon, rinded, grilled
and crumbled
chopped parsley

Slice the cabbage finely. Mix the vinegar with salt, mustard and sweetener to taste; sprinkle over the cabbage. Beat the eggs and milk together and heat, stirring, until just beginning to thicken; pour over the cabbage. Toss lightly and serve sprinkled with the crumbled bacon and chopped parsley.

Spinach slaw

½ lb fresh spinach (200 g)
6 oz white cabbage (150 g)
2 oz raisins (50 g)
4 tbsps lemon juice (60 ml)

3 tbsps salad oil (45 ml)
salt and freshly ground black pepper
caster sugar
1 dessert apple, cored and chopped

(Serves 4)

Remove the coarse stems from the spinach and wash the leaves thoroughly; pat leaves dry. Shred the spinach and trimmed cabbage finely. Soak the raisins in 2 tbsps (30 ml) lemon juice until soft and swollen, then add to the shredded spinach and cabbage. Whisk together the oil, remaining 2 tbsps (30 ml) lemon juice, salt, pepper and sugar to taste. Add the apple. Pour the dressing over the spinach and blend ingredients with 2 forks until glistening.

Slimmer's picnic — pork and liver loaf (*page 119*)

Apricot creams

(see picture page 129)

1½ lb fresh apricots (700 g)
¼ pint water (125 ml)
4–5 saccharin tablets
1 egg
½ pint milk (250 ml)

½ oz powdered gelatine (15 ml)
5 fl oz natural fat-free yoghurt (about 140 ml)
a few blanched pistachios to decorate (optional)

(Serves 4)

Stew the apricots in the water until tender and add sweetener to taste. Strain off the juice, reserve six apricots and sieve the remainder. Chop four of the reserved apricots and divide between four dishes. Make a custard with the egg and milk, mix with the puréed fruit and allow to cool. Dissolve the gelatine in the fruit juice in a small basin over a pan of hot water. Fold the yoghurt into the purée, stir in the gelatine. Pour the mixture over the chopped fruit and chill. Decorate with the remaining apricots, halved, and pistachio nuts, if used.

Plum and orange salad

1 lb red plums (450 g)
2 oranges

liquid sweetener

(Serves 4)

Stone and slice the plums. Add the juice of the oranges and the finely grated rind of half an orange. Add a few drops of sweetener to taste and leave the salad in a cool place for at least 2–3 hours before serving.

Spiced pear grill

1 lb dessert pears, peeled and sliced (450 g)
¼ pint water (125 ml)
finely grated rind of ½ lemon

small piece of cinnamon stick
artificial sweetener
2 oz cornflakes (50 g)
1 oz margarine or butter (25 g)

(Serves 4)

Cook the pears in the water with the lemon rind and the cinnamon. Add sweetener to taste. Place in a shallow flameproof dish, sprinkle with cornflakes and dot with margarine. Place under a moderate grill for 5 minutes.

Banana sherbert

3 bananas, peeled
¼ pint lemon juice (*125 ml*)
½ pint low-fat milk (*250 ml*)

1 pint unsweetened orange juice
  (*500 ml*)
artificial sweetener

(Serves 4)

Mash or blend the bananas with the lemon juice. Add the milk and orange
juice, with sweetener to taste. Freeze for 1 hour, then turn the mixture into a
bowl and beat until smooth. Pour back into the tray and freeze until firm
– overnight if necessary. Spoon into glasses, and decorate with a twist of orange
or lemon peel.

Rhubarb cream

1 lb rhubarb (*450 g*)
¼ pint water (*125 ml*)
artificial sweetener

1 pint fat-free yoghurt (*500 ml*)
toasted almonds to decorate
  (optional)

(Serves 4)

Cut the rhubarb into ½-in (1-cm) lengths and simmer gently in the water for
1–2 minutes, until tender but not mushy. Add the sweetener to taste. Cool.
Blend with the yoghurt and serve in individual glasses, topped if wished with
toasted almonds.

Stuffed cabbage leaves (*page 120*)

Apricot creams (*page 126*)

12 COOKING WITH ZEST

Herbs and spices, indispensable in any kind of imaginative cookery, are doubly important when you are trying to save money by giving a lift to ordinary ingredients. Use fresh herbs if possible. It is economical and practical to grow your own if you can. Even a few flower pots or a small window box can be used for thyme, tarragon, marjoram and chives – and parsley and mint as well, if you like, though mint has a tendency to take over the whole box. A culinary bay tree is decorative as well as useful, and considerably cheaper than the ornamental varieties. If you have to rely on dried herbs, buy the best you can afford and store them in airtight containers. Buy in small quantities so that you can use them before they lose their flavour.

Spices, too, should be treated with care. If you can, buy whole spices (such as peppercorns, coriander seeds and juniper berries) and grind them – using a mill or a pestle and mortar – only when you are going to use them. In addition to 'predictable' spices such as cinnamon and nutmegs, have juniper, allspice and coriander in the cupboard. Juniper berries, crushed, go well with pork and veal and give an interesting flavour to potatoes. (Add a couple to the potatoes as they cook.) Crushed coriander seeds can be added to stuffings for poultry, pâtés and, with garlic and carraway, make a good seasoning for fish. Allspice is good with most meats.

Garlic is another ingredient which gives zest to many things, meat and vegetable. Used with care, it can be so effective that even professed garlic-haters will praise your cooking. (You can, of course, be more lavish if you know you're catering for addicts!) Don't confine garlic to casseroles, dips, and joints of lamb. Try adding some, crushed, to creamed potatoes or to potatoes persillées – slices of boiled potato put in a shallow flameproof dish and sprinkled with a mixture of finely chopped garlic (just a little), parsley and breadcrumbs, mixed with melted margarine. Brown the top under the grill. Or serve boiled new potatoes, or canned potatoes, with garlic flavoured French dressing or a little garlic flavoured mayonnaise. Cooked French beans and chicory are also good with a garlic dressing.

Potatoes and cabbage benefit from a dash of nutmeg or paprika – or try a little curry powder in the mayonnaise for a potato salad. Ginger isn't simply for gingerbread or melon slices; rub it lightly into cod or haddock before grilling or frying, and into pot roasts before browning. Lamb chops and chicken pieces are given a new interest if rubbed with a pepper/ginger seasoning before cooking.

A good way of improving a cheap cut of meat is to marinade it before cooking in vinegar, oil and herbs. Put the meat in the marinade and keep it covered in a cool place, turning frequently. When the marinading is complete, usually after two or three hours, drain off the liquid but keep it either for adding to the gravy or using it to baste the meat as it cooks.

Liver and bacon pudding with herbs

8 oz lean streaky bacon, rinded (*200 g*)
8 oz onions, skinned and chopped
  (*200 g*)
1 lb lamb's or ox liver, chopped (*400 g*)
2 level tbsps flour (*30 ml*)
1 level tbsp tomato paste (*15 ml*)
5 tbsps stock or water (*75 ml*)

salt and pepper
12 oz self-raising flour (*300 g*)
½ level tsp salt (*2.5 ml*)
1½ level tsps dried mixed herbs (*7.5 ml*)
3 oz butter or margarine (*75 g*)
7 fl oz milk, approx. (*200 ml*)

(Serves 6)

Scissor-snip the bacon into a large frying pan and cook over a gentle heat until the fat runs. Add the onion and liver and continue cooking until the onion is transparent. Stir in the flour, tomato paste and stock. Season, bring to the boil, reduce the heat and cook gently for a few minutes. Cool.

Sift the flour and salt together into a basin. Add the herbs and rub the fat into the flour. Stir in enough milk to form a fairly soft dough then roll it out about ¼-in. (½-cm) thick. Using a 2-in. (5-cm) cutter, stamp out 30 rounds to line a 3-pint (1.5-litre) greased ovenproof pudding basin. Slightly overlap each round. Spoon the liver mixture into the centre. Roll out the pastry trimmings for a lid. Bake in the oven at 425 °F (220 °C), mark 7, for 30 minutes then reduce the heat to 375 °F (190 °C), mark 5, for a further 30 minutes. Unmould and serve with a tomato sauce.

Venetian liver

2 oz dripping (*50 g*)
2 large onions (8 oz), skinned and
  chopped (*200 g*)
¾ lb lamb's liver (*300 g*)

2 tbsps chopped parsley (*30 ml*)
juice of 1 lemon
salt and freshly ground black pepper
5 fl oz soured cream (*approx. 120 ml*)

(Serves 3–4)

Melt the dripping in a large frying pan, add the onions and cook until tender, without browning. Cut the liver into thin strips about $2\frac{1}{2}$ in. (6 cm) long; add these to the pan and keep over moderate heat until the liver is cooked through – about 10 minutes. Stir in the parsley and lemon juice. (Don't throw away the rind – it's useful for adding zest to milk puddings and simple cakes.) Adjust the seasoning and re-heat. Serve topped with soured cream, accompanied by boiled rice or pasta and Brussels sprouts.

Kidneys with onion

2 oz dripping (50 g)
4 medium sized onions, skinned and chopped
6 shallots, skinned and chopped
3 tbsps stock (45 ml)

salt and pepper
$1\frac{1}{4}$ lb pig's kidney (500 g)
1 tbsp lemon juice (15 ml)
chopped parsley

(Serves 4–6)

Heat half the dripping in a small pan. Add the onions and shallots and fry until golden brown. Add stock, season and simmer for 20 minutes. Slice the kidney thinly and fry it in the remaining dripping for 15–20 minutes. Sieve the onions and shallots and add the onion purée to the kidney. Reheat and add the lemon juice. Serve sprinkled with chopped parsley.

Colonial goose
(see picture opposite)

4–5 lb leg of lamb, boned (2 kg, approx.)
8 oz sausagemeat (200 g)
4 oz fresh white breadcrumbs (100 g)
1 onion, skinned and finely chopped or grated

salt and pepper
1 clove garlic, skinned and crushed
1 tbsp chopped parsley (15 ml)
1 egg, lightly beaten

(Serves 6–8)

Wipe the leg of lamb. Mix together the sausagemeat, breadcrumbs, onion, seasoning, garlic, parsley and egg. Fill the cavity left by the bone and truss firmly. Place in a baking dish with 1 pint (500 ml) water and cook at 350 °F (180 °C), mark 4, allowing 25–35 minutes per lb (450 g).

132

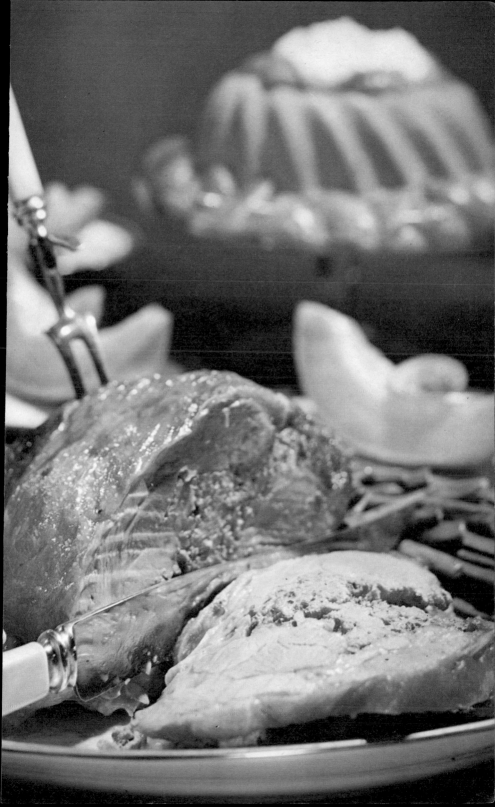

Spiced shoulder of lamb

1 boned shoulder of lamb
1 level tbsp fresh rosemary (15 ml)
2 level tbsps brown sugar (30 ml)
1 level tbsp flour (15 ml)
1 level tsp salt (5 ml)
½ level tsp ground allspice (2.5 ml)

½ level tsp ground ginger (2.5 ml)
pinch nutmeg
2 oz margarine (50 g)
1 tbsp vinegar (15 ml)
1 level tbsp tomato ketchup (15 ml)

(Serves 4)

Flatten the lamb; make slits in the flesh and skin and insert spikes of rosemary
Combine the remaining ingredients and spread half over the fleshy surface
Roll up neatly and tie with fine string. Place the lamb in a roasting tin, pou
the remaining spice mixture over and bake in the oven at 350 °F (180 °C)
mark 4, for about 1½ hours. Serve cold with mint jelly.

Devilled pork

1 lb belly of pork (450 g)
2 level tbsps tomato ketchup (30 ml)
1 tbsp Worcestershire sauce (15 ml)
1 tbsp vinegar (15 ml)

1 tsp thin honey (5 ml)
salt and freshly ground black pepper
½ level tsp made mustard (2.5 ml)
pinch of dried sage

(Serves 4)

Buy the pork ready sliced, or with a sharp knife slice the whole piece evenl·
in eight. Remove the rind and any bones. Combine the remaining ingredients
Brush this mixture over the slices of pork and place them in a single layer in ₴
shallow ovenproof dish, pouring any extra sauce over. Cover with foil and cool
at 400 °F (200 °C), mark 6, for about 40 minutes. Remove the meat and keep
hot. Spoon off any excess fat. Reduce the remaining juices by fast boiling in ₴
pan, then pour the glaze over the pork. Serve with lightly cooked shreddec
cabbage and floury potatoes.

Spiced drumsticks

6 chicken drumsticks (4 oz each)
   (100 g each)
1 oz seasoned flour (25 g)
1 tbsp cooking oil (15 ml)
1 oz butter or margarine (25 g)
2 oz onion, skinned and finely
   chopped (50 g)

1 level tsp curry powder (5 ml)
15-oz can apricot halves (approx. 425 g
5 whole cloves
1½ tbsps lemon juice (20 ml)
¼ pint chicken stock (150 ml)

(Serves 3)

134

redge the drumsticks with flour. Heat the oil in a thick based frying pan, dd the butter and when on the point of browning add the drumsticks. Fry ntil evenly browned then transfer them to a casserole. Sauté the onion in the an juices until it begins to brown; stir in the excess flour with the curry owder, sliced apricots, the juice, cloves, lemon juice and stock. Bring to the oil, stirring and pour over the drumsticks. Cover and cook in the oven at 25 °F (170 °C), mark 3, for about 2 hours. Arrange the drumsticks on a serving late. Reduce the juice to a glaze consistency by boiling if necessary; spoon ver the drumsticks. Serve with plain boiled rice.

Chilli con carne

2 oz haricot or butter beans (300 g)
inch of bicarbonate of soda
½ lb raw minced beef (700 g)
tbsp fat or cooking oil (15 ml)
large onion, skinned and chopped
green pepper, seeded and chopped
(optional)

15-oz can tomatoes (approx. 425 g)
salt and pepper
1–2 level tsps chilli seasoning (5–10 ml)
1 tbsp vinegar (15 ml)
1 level tsp sugar (5 ml)

Serves 4–6)

oak the beans overnight in cold water with the bicarbonate of soda. Fry the eef in the fat or oil until lightly browned, then add the onion and pepper nd fry for a further 5 minutes, until soft. Stir in the beans and tomatoes and dd the seasoning and chilli seasoning blended with the vinegar and sugar. Cover and simmer for 2–2½ hours, or until tender.
Note: Traditionally, red kidney beans should be used; if you want to use them nstead of haricot or butter beans, add the contents of a 15-oz (425-g) can 10 ninutes before the cooking time is completed.

Spaghetti bolognese

see picture page 136)

1 lb minced beef (450 g)
1 oz butter or margarine (25 g)
¼ lb mushrooms, sliced, optional
(100 g)
6 oz onions, skinned and chopped
(150 g)
½ level tsp dried fines herbes or
marjoram (2.5 ml)

1 bayleaf
1 level tbsp flour (15 ml)
4 tbsps water (60 ml)
1 beef stock cube
14-oz can tomatoes (approx. 396 g)
1 level tbsp tomato paste (15 ml)

Serves 4)

In a saucepan, slowly fry the beef in half the butter or margarine until begin-

135

ning to brown. Turn out of the saucepan. To the pan add remaining butte
or margarine and fry the sliced mushrooms for 5 minutes. Drain from the fa
and keep on one side. Reheat the fat, add the onions and cook until beginning
to brown. Stir in the *fines herbes* or marjoram, the bayleaf, flour and mince
Slowly add the water, crumbled beef cube, tomatoes and paste. Bring to the
boil, stir, reduce the heat and simmer, covered, for 30 minutes. Stir in the
mushrooms and cook for a further 5 minutes. To serve, cook 6–8 oz (150–
200 g) spaghetti in boiling salted water; drain well. Pile the spaghetti on indi
vidual plates and spoon the sauce over. Hand freshly grated Parmesan cheese
separately.

Veal casserole

2 lb stewing veal (*1 kg*)
salt and pepper
1 oz plain flour (*25 g*)
1 oz margarine (*25 g*)
2 tbsps cooking oil (*30 ml*)
1 clove garlic, skinned and finely
   chopped
2½-oz can tomato paste (*approx. 70 g*)

1 pint beef stock, made with a cube
   (*550 ml*)
bayleaf
pinch of thyme
pinch of marjoram
4 oz mushrooms, sliced (*100 g*)

(Serves 6–8)

Spaghetti bolognese (*page 135*)

Sweet-sour red cabbage (*page 139*)

Cut the veal into cubes. Dip the meat in seasoned flour and brown in margarine and oil, together with the garlic. Add the tomato paste and boiling stock, also the herbs and some seasoning. Cook for 1½ hours at 350 °F (180 °C), mark 4. Half an hour before the end of cooking time, add the mushrooms. Serve with fluffy white rice.

Lemon-stuffed roast veal

3 lb breast of veal, boned weight
  (1.5 kg)
salt and freshly ground black pepper
3 tbsps lemon juice (45 ml)
1 oz fresh white breadcrumbs,
  toasted (25 g)
1 level tsp dried rosemary (5 ml)
1 tbsp chopped parsley (15 ml)

1 clove garlic, skinned and crushed
1 oz butter or margarine,
  melted (25 g)
1 egg, beaten
4 thin slices of lemon
4 rashers streaky bacon, rinded
1 tbsp cooking oil (15 ml)

(Serves 6–7)

Flatten out the meat and season with salt, pepper and 1 tbsp (15 ml) lemon juice. In a bowl, combine the breadcrumbs, rosemary, parsley, garlic, melted butter and egg. Season well and, using a palette knife, fill the pocket in the meat with stuffing and spread any remaining stuffing over the meat. With scissors, remove the rind from the lemon slices; arrange the fruit down the centre. Roll up, secure at intervals with string and lay the bacon across the meat. Place the oil and remaining lemon juice in a casserole just large enough to take the joint. Place the meat on top, cover, and roast in the oven at 350 °F (180 °C), mark 4, for about 3½ hours, or until tender. Baste occasionally. Carve and serve hot, or allow to go cold before slicing.

Savoury onion bread

1 level tsp sugar (5 ml)
½ pint tepid water (300 ml)
2 level tsps dried yeast (10 ml)
2 level tbsps dried onion flakes (30 ml)
1 lb strong plain flour (500 g)

2 level tsps salt (10 ml)
½ oz lard (13 g)
beaten egg
mixed herbs

(Makes 8 rolls)

Dissolve the sugar in warm water, sprinkle the yeast and onion flakes on top and leave in a warm place for 10 minutes, or until frothy. Sift the flour and salt into a bowl, rub in the lard, make a well in the centre and pour in the yeast liquid. Work to a firm dough, adding a further 2 tbsps (30 ml) tepid water if needed, until the dough leaves the sides of the bowl. Turn out the dough and knead on a lightly floured surface until smooth – about 10 minutes. Shape into a ball and place in a lightly oiled polythene bag. Tie loosely and leave to rise in a warm place until double in size and springy to the touch – about 1 hour. Knead again briefly, then divide into eight; shape into 8 plaited rolls. Place the rolls on a baking sheet, brush them with beaten egg and sprinkle with herbs. Leave to prove, lightly covered with oiled polythene, in a warm place for about 15 minutes. Bake at 450 °F (230 °C), mark 8, for about 30 minutes. Serve fresh.

Sweet-sour red cabbage

(see picture page 137)

2 lb red cabbage (1 kg)
2 medium sized onions, skinned and
  sliced
2 cooking apples, peeled, cored and
  chopped
2 level tsps sugar (10 ml)

salt and pepper
bouquet garni
2 tbsps water (30 ml)
2 tbsps red wine vinegar (30 ml)
1 oz margarine or butter (25 g)

(Serves 4–6 as an accompaniment)

Shred the cabbage finely, discarding any discoloured outside leaves or coarse stems. Layer the cabbage in a casserole with onions, apples, sugar, and seasoning. Put the bouquet garni in the centre and pour the water and vinegar over. Cover tightly and cook in the oven at 300 °F (150 °C), mark 1–2, for 1 hour. Put the cabbage in the coolest part of oven and continue cooking at 350 °F (180 °C), mark 4, for a further 1½ hours. Add butter or margarine and mix with the cabbage at end of cooking time. This is excellent with pork.

Simple marinades

For beef
¼ pint cooking oil (150 ml)
⅛ pint vinegar (75 ml)
2 level tsps made mustard (10 ml)
herbs as desired

For veal
½ pint tarragon vinegar (300 ml)
¼ pint cooking oil (150 ml)
½ bayleaf

For pork
1 onion, skinned and finely sliced
1 bayleaf
6 peppercorns
juice of 1 lemon
4 tbsps cooking oil (60 ml)

For lamb
2 tbsps salad oil (30 ml)
2 tbsps vinegar or lemon juice (30 ml)
thin slices of onion and carrot
lemon rind
salt
6 peppercorns
2 cloves
parsley sprig
sprig of thyme
bayleaf

For bacon
1 level tsp ground mixed spice (5 ml)
sprig of parsley
pinch of basil
¼ pint cider (150 ml)
⅛ pint corn oil (75 ml)

13 FINISHING TOUCHES

When you've gone to the trouble of making a delicious money-saving meal, enhance the effect – and your reputation – by attractive presentation. Finishing touches can make such a difference – providing they are not just inedible and unrelated extras. Never try to disguise a dish by too much garnish and don't add so much that service is slowed up and the food is chilled.

Choose a garnish that adds texture, flavour, colour or contrast. Crisp golden buttered crumbs on macaroni cheese, savoury butter – or margarine – on a plain grilled cod cutlet, or tomato sauce with stuffed marrow, are all easily produced and do enhance the food they garnish. The most useful garnish of all, perhaps, is parsley, whether in sprigs, or finely chopped. But be careful not to overdo it!

From an economical and practical point of view it is sensible to choose a garnish which can be made from part of the main ingredients. If you are using lemon juice or rind in a dish, for instance, keep back a couple of slices. If peas or green peppers are included, use these in the same way.

Sweet dishes may not need much garnishing; hot puddings may require nothing more than a light dusting of fine sugar or a sauce. Be careful not to overdress cold desserts; but if you are topping them with a swirl of whipped cream, use a nozzle with a large aperture for piping. This will look better, and cream piped through a narrow aperture could in any case be ruined. If you think a dessert would benefit from an extra touch, but don't know what to add, try grated chocolate, or chocolate vermicelli, crushed brandysnaps, or toasted almonds. Of course, if you buy specially these decorations are expensive, but you may have enough in the cupboard left over from some other dish.

Presentation and serving
You can carry your economising right into the presentation of food by using slightly smaller plates than usual – a fish plate instead of a dinner plate, for instance, will look fuller and the psychological effect on the eater is likely to be

Extras for desserts (*page 145*)

A swirl of cream for each serving

that he will think he is eating more than he really is! Conversely, adequate servings on a large plate may well give the diner the impression that he being underfed. The simplest food, if attractively presented, gets the warmes welcome. Why spend hours making a mixed salad into a symmetrically de signed centrepiece which nobody dares to touch, let alone eat? It is better t arrange the ingredients naturally, or toss them lightly in dressing and serv with some scissor-snipped chives. Dish up hot food neatly and quickly an serve it at once.

Hints
To remove brown rivulets from the side of a casserole, use a damp cloth wit a dab of salt.

Always taste such dishes as soups and stews and adjust the seasoning necessary; but unless you are sure of the eaters' tastes it is better to unde season than to use too much salt and pepper.

Skim off any fat layer from stews, soups and casseroles by drawing a piec of absorbent paper across the surface.

Hot foods should usually be served piping hot and cold foods quite col but there are exceptions. Pastry flans, etc., are best at room temperature rathe than chilled, and foods which hold the heat – such as mincemeat, treacl tart and apple and toffee sauces – should be warm rather than hot.

Pile up the food in the dish rather than have it flat; it is easier to handl and looks more tempting. If you are arranging a cold platter, give height t sliced meats with a frame of crumpled kitchen foil; the meats themselves ca be folded or twisted to give more height.

If you are coating fish or chicken portions with sauce before serving, use th broad side of the spoon for pouring, giving just a film. Serve the rest of th sauce separately.

A little sauce spooned into the dish before you arrange, say, cutlets, help to prevent them slipping about.

If foods need reheating, heat them separately rather than together; a sauc can then be safely stirred without breaking up tender pieces of fish, chicken or other ingredients.

Extras for soups, casseroles and au gratin dishes
Slivered salted almonds and peanuts, garlic croûtons, minced parsley, chive or celery leaves.

For creamy vegetable or chicken soup:
Carrot curls: Use a potato peeler to pare off long thin slivers from the outside Blanch in boiling salted water for 2 minutes. Drain well, curl into a 'snail shape and cool.

For soups, seafood casseroles and chicken fricassees:
Fleurons: Roll out puff pastry thinly and stamp out rounds using a $1\frac{1}{2}$-in (3-cm) fluted cutter. Brush with beaten egg, fold over into semi-circles anc place on a baking sheet. Glaze the tops with beaten egg and sprinkle witl

142

ppy seeds. Leave in a cool place for about 30 minutes. Bake in the oven at 00 °F (200 °C), mark 6, for about 15 minutes. Serve warm. (If made in dvance, reheat in the oven.)

With fried fish, beef stews, cream of onion soup (float on top at the last minute)
onion rings: Slice not-too-large onions $\frac{1}{4}$ in. (0.5 cm) thick and separate into rings. Dip in fritter batter and deep fry at 375 °F (190 °C) a few at a time until golden – about 3–4 minutes.

For most soups, as an alternative to croûtons:
deep-fried croûtes: Use a freshly-baked pre-sliced loaf. Stamp out an even number of rounds with a $1\frac{1}{2}$-in. (4-cm) fluted cutter and remove the centres with a plain or fluted $\frac{3}{4}$-in. (2-cm) cutter to make rings. For entwined bread rings, break one circle and slip another through, sealing the break by pressing together firmly (this is why you need really fresh bread). Deep fat fry at 375 °F (190 °C) till crisp and golden brown. Drain on absorbent paper. Serve fresh.

For clear soups:
choux puffs: Pipe small blobs of basic choux pastry, using a $\frac{3}{4}$-in. (2-cm) plain nozzle, on to a greased baking sheet. Sprinkle with grated Parmesan or Cheddar cheese before baking at 425 °F (200 °C), mark 6, for about 20 minutes.

For main-meal soups like lentil, corn chowder, or old-fashioned vegetable:
sausage floats: You need 8 skinless sausages, 1 small egg, hardboiled and finely chopped or sieved, 1 level tbsp (15 ml) flour, 1 level tbsp (15 ml) thick mayonnaise and $\frac{1}{2}$ level tbsp (7.5 ml) dry mustard, plus seasoning. Work together the egg, flour, mayonnaise, mustard and seasoning. Place three sausages in the palm of your hand so that the middle one sits slightly lower than the other two. Pile or pipe the egg mixture along the centre to form a core, then put two more sausages on top. (The remaining three sausages can be used to make a smaller version, with two sausages as the base and one on top.) Secure with fine string three or four times and bake in the oven at 400 °F (200 °C), mark 6, for about 20 minutes. Drain well and chill. Remove the string and slice thinly. Float on top of soup.

Other ideas for soups

Bacon: Rind some lean rashers of bacon, cut into small strips or dice and fry lightly. Good for thick soups. Alternatively, grill the bacon until just crisp, crumble roughly and sprinkle over the soup.

Cheese: Use hard cheese and grate it freshly for a pleasant addition to a vegetable soup. It is usually served separately, but may also be sprinkled on the soup just before it is served. A little chopped fresh herb such as parsley may be mixed with the cheese for added colour. Cut-outs of processed cheese also go well with tomato soup.

Sausagemeat: Left-over cooked sausages go well with vegetable soups such as spinach. Cut sausages into rounds and heat in the soup. Make sausagemeat into small balls and simmer in the soup for 20 minutes.

For fish

Lemon butterflies: Cut thin slices of lemon and divide each in half. Take one half and divide the rind and membrane at midpoint but without cutting right through to the centre. Open out to give the winged effect.

For salads

Deckled or ridged cucumber: Take a piece of washed cucumber and score the skin lengthwise with the prongs of a fork. When the cucumber is sliced, each piece will have a crinkled or deckled edge. Use in green salads, etc.

Cucumber cones: Cut thin slices of cucumber. Make a cut in each slice from the centre to the outer edge, then wrap one cut edge over the other to form a cone.

Celery curls: Cut a celery stick into strips about $\frac{1}{2}$ in. (1 cm) wide and 2 in. (4 cm) long. Make cuts along the length of each, close together and to within $\frac{1}{2}$ in. (1 cm) of one end. Leave the pieces in cold or iced water for 1–2 hours, until the fringed strips curl. Drain well before using.

Gherkin fans: Choose long, thin, whole gherkins. Cut each lengthwise into thin slices, leaving them joined at one end. Fan out the strips of gherkin so that they overlap each other.

Radish roses: Trim the radishes; make 4 or 8 small, deep cuts, crossing in the centre at the root end. Leave the radishes in cold or iced water for 1–2 hours, till the cuts open to form 'petals'.

Tomato lilies: Choose firm, even-sized tomatoes. Using a small, sharp pointed knife, make a series of V-shaped cuts round the middle of each tomato, cutting right through to the centre. Carefully pull the halves apart.

For desserts

Home-made or bought whips, served in individual glasses, fruit soufflés and mousses are more attractive if the decoration is simple. Use crushed or whole small brandy snaps, whirls of piped cream, chocolate coarsely grated or curled, roughly chopped nuts, crushed caramel, coconut – toasted, desiccated or long-shred.

Frosted grapes: Wash and dry grapes in groups of three, or pairs, or singly. (Use black or white, or both.) Brush evenly with egg white, then dip in caster sugar to coat. Leave to dry thoroughly, overnight if possible.

Chocolate almonds: Melt a little plain chocolate cake covering. Dip whole or halved blanched almonds in the chocolate to half-coat. Allow the excess to drip off and leave to set on non-stick paper. Keep in a cool place.

Praline leaves: Put $5\frac{1}{2}$ oz (140 g) caster sugar in a heavy-based pan, and dissolve over a low heat. When a deep caramel colour, add 4 oz (100 g) nibbed almonds a little at a time, stirring with a metal spoon. Turn quickly on to a clean oiled baking sheet, or marble surface, and, using a whole lemon, roll out the praline thinly. With warm cutters, stamp out into leaf shapes. If the praline sets too quickly, return to the warm oven for a few minutes. These can be stored, when cooled, for several days in an airtight tin. The trimmings can also be crushed and used as a garnish.

Salad garnishes

Sugar crisps: Using fairly soft royal icing, pipe 1–1½ in. (2–3 cm) diameter discs freehand on to a foil-lined baking sheet. Dry for about 1 hour. Place under a low grill, still on the foil, for about 10 minutes, until dried and pale brown. They should slip off the foil easily when ready. Turn them over and dry a little longer. Cool before storing. These will keep for up to a week in an airtight container.

Chocolate leaves: Melt some chocolate in a basin over hot water. Choose various sized rose leaves, each with a stem. Using tweezers, draw the underside of each leaf across the melted chocolate. Leave on waxed paper, chocolate side up, until set. Peel off the leaf from the stem end, carefully easing it away. Keep the leaves in a cool place until required; use to decorate a cake or cold sweet, such as a mousse.

Chocolate squares and triangles: Pour melted chocolate in a thin layer on to non-stick paper placed on a baking sheet. When set, cut with a sharp knife to give small shapes, which can be used to decorate cold sweets, cakes and buns.

For decorating pies

Pastry leaves: Cut a narrow strip of pastry, then cut across with diagonal lines to give diamond shapes. Mark the veins with a knife.

Pastry tassel: (for raised veal and ham pies). Cut an oblong pastry strip and cut at close intervals, leaving an uncut band along one edge. Roll up the strip and damp the end of the uncut part to make it stick. Before fixing to the pie, separate out the fringe.

14 SAUCES AND DRESSINGS

If you feel that plainly cooked meat or fish needs something extra, don't just reach for the bottle of bought fruit sauce or tomato ketchup. Make your own – not necessarily the kind that takes time in preparation and then long simmering on the cooker, but something just as interesting and more quickly prepared.

The same applies to sweet sauces, too, for ice creams and steamed puddings; it is useful to have some ready-made varieties on the shelf, but even more useful to have recipes for some you can make yourself. If you have never made your own chutneys and pickles, do try – you can hardly go wrong. Although home-made pickles often commend themselves to housewives because of their cheapness and the way they make use of readily available ingredients such as an over-abundance of apples, green tomatoes or rhubarb, there's no denying that it's the flavour that commends them to the eater. Make as much as you can and store (and/or give away) what isn't required at once.

Pease pudding

½ lb green split peas (200 g)
1 medium sized onion, skinned and
    roughly sliced
water

1 oz margarine (25 g)
1 egg, beaten
salt, pepper and grated nutmeg

Wash the peas and soak them overnight. Drain and put them in a saucepan with the onion and add water just to cover. Boil, reduce heat, then cover and simmer for about 2 hours until the peas are soft and the water is absorbed (or you can drain off the excess). Crush the peas against the side of the pan with a wooden spoon to see if they are cooked. Purée the mixture, return it to the pan and add the margarine, egg and seasoning. Reheat, stirring. If a bacon joint is simmering at the same time, the peas can be cooked along with it, the old way, tied in a well greased pudding cloth, with pepper and nutmeg but no salt – this is supplied by the bacon.

Barbecue sauce

2 oz butter or margarine (*50 g*)
1 large onion, skinned and chopped
1 level tsp tomato paste (*5 ml*)
2 tbsps vinegar (*30 ml*)

2 level tbsps Demerara sugar (*30 ml*)
2 level tsps dry mustard (*10 ml*)
2 tbsps Worcestershire sauce (*30 ml*)
¼ pint water (*150 ml*)

Melt the butter or margarine and fry the onion for 5 minutes or until soft
Stir in the tomato paste and continue cooking for a further 3 minutes. Blenc
the remaining ingredients to a smooth cream and stir in the onion mixture
Return the sauce to the pan and simmer for 10 minutes. Serve with chicken
sausages, hamburgers or chops.

Red tomato chutney

4 lb red tomatoes, skinned (*1.8 kg*)
1 oz mustard seed (*25 g*)
3 tsps whole allspice (*15 ml*)
1 level tsp cayenne pepper (*5 ml*)

½ lb sugar (*200 g*)
1 oz salt (*25 g*)
¾ pint white vinegar (*375 ml*)

(Makes about 3 lb) (*1 kg*)

Chop the tomatoes roughly and put them in a large pan. Tie the mustard seec
and allspice in muslin and add, with the cayenne, to the tomatoes. Simmer
until reduced to a pulp – about 45 minutes; add the remaining ingredients
Continue simmering until of a thick consistency, with no excess liquid. Pot anc
cover with vinegar-proof parchment.

Apple chutney

3 lb cooking apples, peeled, cored and
   diced (*1 kg*)
3 lb onions, skinned and chopped (*1 kg*)
1 lb sultanas or stoned raisins (*450 g*)

2 lemons
1½ lb Demerara sugar (*500 g*)
1 pint vinegar (*400 ml*)

(Makes approximately 4 lb) (*1.5 kg*)

Put the apples, onions and sultanas in a pan. Grate the lemon rind, strain the
juice and add both to the pan with the sugar and vinegar. Bring to the boil
reduce the heat and simmer until the mixture is of a thick consistency, with
no excess liquid. Pot and cover with vinegar-proof parchment. This chutney
is good with pork and poultry.

Rhubarb chutney

3 lb rhubarb cut small (1.2 kg)
8 oz seedless raisins (200 g)
 oz ground ginger (10 ml)
½ pints vinegar (700 ml)
1 lb tomatoes, skinned and
 chopped (400 g)

4 oz onions, skinned and
 chopped (100 g)
1 oz mustard seed (25 g)
1 oz salt (25 g)
1 lb 8 oz Demerara sugar (600 g)

Put all the ingredients except the sugar into a pan. Bring to the boil. Turn off the heat, stir in the sugar until dissolved, then return to the boil. Boil gently for about 1½ hours until thick. If the mixture splashes too much, cover the pan loosely with foil. When it becomes thick, spoon into sterilised jars and cover with vinegar-proof parchment.

Marrow chutney

3 lb marrow, peeled and seeded (1.2 kg)
salt
8 oz shallots, skinned and sliced (200 g)
8 oz apples, peeled, cored and
 sliced (200 g)

12 peppercorns
4 oz dried whole root ginger (100 g)
8 oz sultanas (200 g)
4 oz Demerara sugar (100 g)
1½ pints vinegar (850 ml)

Cut the marrow into small pieces and place in a bowl. Sprinkle liberally with salt. Cover and leave for 12 hours, then drain well and place in a pan with the shallots and apples. Tie the peppercorns and ginger in muslin; put in the pan with the sultanas, sugar and vinegar. Bring to the boil, reduce the heat and simmer uncovered until the consistency is thick, with no excess liquid. Pot and cover with vinegar-proof parchment.

Ketchup dip

½ lb cottage cheese (200 g)
1 small onion, skinned and finely
 chopped
4 level tbsps tomato ketchup (60 ml)
1 level tsp made mustard (5 ml)

1 clove garlic, skinned and crushed
salt and freshly ground black pepper
½ pint cream or top of the milk (200 ml)
¼ level tsp cayenne pepper (1.25 ml)

Mix all ingredients together to form a smooth mixture and chill before serving.

Oriental dip

8 oz cream cheese (200 g)
2 tbsps single cream (30 ml)
2 tsps soy sauce (10 ml)
2 tsps onion juice (10 ml)

1 tsp lemon juice (5 ml)
¼ level tsp ground ginger (1.25 ml)
1 oz nibbed almonds, toasted
   (optional) (25 g)

Mix the cheese, cream, soy sauce, juices and ginger to a smooth consistency.
Chill. Serve topped with almonds, if used.

Redcurrant relish

Finely chop some fresh mint to give about 2 tbsps (30 ml); stir in ¼ lb (100 g)
redcurrant jelly. This relish is delicious with lamb.

Quince cheese

3 lb quinces (1.5 kg)
water

1 lb sugar to each lb pulp (1 kg to each
   kg pulp)

Wash and chop the quinces, without peeling or coring. Put them in a pan.
Add sufficient water to cover the fruit and then simmer gently for about 30
minutes, or until really soft. Sieve and weigh the pulp, then return it to the
pan with the sugar. Stir until dissolved, then boil gently until thick, stirring
regularly. Pot in small straight-sided jars, brushed inside with a little glycerine
if you want to turn the cheeses out whole. Cover as for jam. Keep for at least
3–4 months before eating, to develop the flavour.
   Serve as a dessert – studded with split almonds (and with port poured over) –
or as an accompaniment for meat, poultry or game.

Pickled prunes

2 lb prunes (800 g)
1 lb sugar (400 g)
¾ pint vinegar (400 ml)
thinly pared rind of ¼ lemon

2 whole cloves
¼ oz whole allspice (15 ml)
small piece root ginger
piece of cinnamon stick

(Makes about 2 lb) (about 800 g)

Soak the prunes overnight; prick the skins with a pin. Dissolve the sugar in
the vinegar and add the flavouring ingredients. Add the drained fruit and boil

ently for about 15 minutes. Pack the prunes into hot jars and discard the flavourings. Boil the vinegar until syrupy and pour over the prunes to fill the jars. Seal with vinegar-proof parchment. Excellent with roast pork or turkey.

Spiced pears

2 lb firm eating pears (800 g)
½ pint cider vinegar (400 ml)
½ pint water (250 ml)
1 lb sugar (400 g)

1 cinnamon stick, broken in half
10 whole cloves
small piece root ginger

Peel, core and quarter the pears. Place in a pan and cover with boiling water. Cook gently until almost tender. Drain. Boil together for 5 minutes the cider vinegar, ½ pint water, sugar, cinnamon, cloves and root ginger. Add the pears and cook until clear. Drain the pears and pack them into hot jars, cover with boiling syrup and seal with vinegar-proof parchment. Serve with slices of gammon.

Beetroot relish

2¾ lb sugar (1 kg)
¾ pint vinegar (400 ml)

1 lb cooked beetroot, peeled (400 g)
1 bottle commercial pectin, e.g. Certo

Measure the sugar and vinegar into a saucepan. Coarsely grate or finely chop the beetroot, add to the pan and heat slowly until the sugar has dissolved. Bring to the boil and boil rapidly for 2 minutes. Remove from the heat and stir in the pectin. Stir and skim for just 5 minutes. Pot in small jars and cover as for jam.

Jam sauce

6 level tbsps strawberry jam (100 ml)
¾ pint water (400 ml)
4 strips lemon rind
2 level tbsps sugar (30 ml)

¼ level tsp ground cinnamon (1.25 ml)
2 level tbsps arrowroot (30 ml)
juice of 1 lemon

Mix the jam, water and lemon rind in a saucepan. In a basin, combine the sugar and cinnamon; add to the contents of the pan, heat and bring to the boil. Cook steadily for 2–3 minutes then remove from the heat. Blend the arrowroot with the lemon juice, add to the pan and reheat for a few minutes until thickened. Strain before serving.

Apple and raisin sauce

½ oz butter or margarine (*about 15 g*)
1 lb cooking apples, peeled, cored
   and sliced (*450 g*)
pared rind of ½ lemon

3 oz caster sugar (*75 g*)
¼ pint water (*150 ml*)
2 oz seedless raisins (*50 g*)

Melt the butter in a medium sized pan and swirl it round to coat the sides
Add the apples and lemon rind, cover with the lid and cook gently to a soft
pulp. Rub through a nylon sieve. Dissolve the sugar in the water and boil for
3–4 minutes, until a thick syrup. Stir in the pulp and the raisins. Simmer for
a few minutes more. Serve hot with rice and other cereal puddings.

Marshmallow sauce

4 oz sugar (*100 g*)
3 tbsps water (*45 ml*)
8 marshmallows, cut up small

1 egg white
½ tsp vanilla essence (*2.5 ml*)
few drops of red colouring, optional

Dissolve the sugar in water and boil for 5 minutes. Add the marshmallows
and stir until melted. Whip the egg white stiffly and gradually fold in the
marshmallow mixture. Flavour with vanilla and tint pink, if desired. Serve
over coffee or chocolate ice cream.

Lemon sauce

grated rind and juice of 1 large lemon
3 level tbsps caster sugar (*45 ml*)
1 oz butter or margarine (*25 g*)

½ oz cornflour (*25 ml*)
½ pint water (*300 ml*)
1 egg yolk

Blend the lemon rind with the sugar. In a saucepan, melt the butter or
margarine and stir in the cornflour, then gradually add the water. Stir continuously until boiling, then simmer for 2–3 minutes. Add the rind, sugar
and strained juice. Remove the pan from the heat and quickly stir in the egg
yolk. Serve at once.

Butterscotch sauce

2 oz butter or margarine (*50 g*)
2 oz soft brown sugar (*50 g*)

2 level tbsps golden syrup (*30 ml*)
squeeze of lemon juice

Sauces and seasonings can make a dish

Warm the butter, sugar and syrup in a saucepan until well blended. Boil for a minute, then stir in the lemon juice.

Chocolate peppermint sauce

8 oz chocolate peppermint creams
(200 g)

6-oz can evaporated milk (*150 g*)
1 oz butter or margarine (*25 g*)

Break up the chocolate creams and put into a saucepan with the milk. Stir over a gentle heat until melted. When hot, add the butter or margarine and stir. Serve immediately.

Pineapple sauce

4 oz sugar (*100 g*)
¼ pint water (*150 ml*)
2 level tbsps apricot jam, sieved (*30 ml*)
2–3 tsps lemon juice (*10 ml*)

2 level tbsps shredded
  pineapple (*30 ml*)
2 level tsps cornflour (*10 ml*)
few drops yellow colouring, optional

Dissolve the sugar in the water in a small saucepan. Add the apricot jam, lemon juice and pineapple. Blend the cornflour with a little cold water and add it to the pan, stirring. Bring to the boil, still stirring. Add a little yellow colouring if you wish.

Chocolate sauce

½ oz cocoa powder (*20 ml*)
2 oz caster sugar (*50 g*)
1 oz butter or margarine (*25 g*)
1 tsp vanilla essence (*5 ml*)

1 tbsp coffee essence (*15 ml*)
4 tbsps milk (*60 ml*)
2 tbsps golden syrup (*30 ml*)

Combine the cocoa powder and caster sugar. Melt butter or margarine in a pan, add cocoa, sugar, vanilla essence, coffee essence and milk. Heat together to dissolve the sugar and to cook the cocoa. Stir in the golden syrup. Increase the heat and boil for 1–2 minutes before serving.

INDEX